Connected  Mathematics™

Covering and Surrounding

Two-Dimensional Measurement

Teacher's Edition

Glenda Lappan
James T. Fey
William M. Fitzgerald
Susan N. Friel
Elizabeth Difanis Phillips

Developed at Michigan State University

DALE SEYMOUR PUBLICATIONS®
WHITE PLAINS, NEW YORK

Connected Mathematics™ was developed at Michigan State University with financial support from the Michigan State University Office of the Provost, Computing and Technology, and the College of Natural Science.

This material is based upon work supported by the National Science Foundation under Grant No. MDR 9150217.

This project was supported, in part,
by the
National Science Foundation
Opinions expressed are those of the authors
and not necessarily those of the Foundation

The Michigan State University authors and administration have agreed that all MSU royalties arising from this publication will be devoted to purposes supported by the Department of Mathematics and the MSU Mathematics Education Enrichment Fund.

This book is published by Dale Seymour Publications®, an imprint of Addison Wesley Longman, Inc.

> Dale Seymour Publications
> 10 Bank Street
> White Plains, NY 10602
> Customer Service: 800 872-1100

Managing Editor: Catherine Anderson
Project Editor: Stacey Miceli
Book Editor: Mali Apple
Revision Editor: James P. McAuliffe
ESL Consultant: Nancy Sokol Green
Production/Manufacturing Director: Janet Yearian
Production/Manufacturing Coordinators: Claire Flaherty, Alan Noyes
Design Manager: John F. Kelly
Photo Editor: Roberta Spieckerman
Design: Don Taka
Composition: London Road Design, Palo Alto, CA
Electronic Prepress Revision: A. W. Kingston Publishing Services, Chandler, AZ
Illustrations: Pauline Phung, Margaret Copeland, Ray Godfrey
Cover: Ray Godfrey

Photo Acknowledgements: 6 © Hazel Hankin/Stock, Boston; 7© Hamilton Smith/FPG International; 19 © Michael Tamborrino/FPG International; 22 © Toyohiro Yamada/FPG International; 25 © Ira Kirschenbaum/Stock, Boston; 29 © George Bellerose/Stock, Boston; 35 © Walter Sittig/The Image Works; 38 © Carrie Boretz/The Image Works; 59 © William B. Finch/Stock, Boston; 69 (umbrellas) © Owen Franken/Stock, Boston; 69 (manhole) © Peter Vandermark/Stock, Boston; 69 (dog) © Peter Southwick/Stock, Boston; 70 © Barbara Alper/Stock, Boston; 75 © Mark Antman/The Image Works

Order number 45814
ISBN 1-57232-619-0

2 3 4 5 6 7 8 9 10-ML-01 00 99 98

The Connected Mathematics Project Staff

Project Directors

James T. Fey
University of Maryland

William M. Fitzgerald
Michigan State University

Susan N. Friel
University of North Carolina at Chapel Hill

Glenda Lappan
Michigan State University

Elizabeth Difanis Phillips
Michigan State University

Project Manager

Kathy Burgis
Michigan State University

Technical Coordinator

Judith Martus Miller
Michigan State University

Collaborating Teachers/Writers

Mary K. Bouck
Portland, Michigan

Jacqueline Stewart
Okemos, Michigan

Curriculum Development Consultants

David Ben-Chaim
Weizmann Institute

Alex Friedlander
Weizmann Institute

Eleanor Geiger
University of Maryland

Jane Mitchell
University of North Carolina at Chapel Hill

Anthony D. Rickard
Alma College

Evaluation Team

Mark Hoover
Michigan State University

Diane V. Lambdin
Indiana University

Sandra K. Wilcox
Michigan State University

Judith S. Zawojewski
National-Louis University

Graduate Assistants

Scott J. Baldridge
Michigan State University

Angie S. Eshelman
Michigan State University

M. Faaiz Gierdien
Michigan State University

Jane M. Keiser
Indiana University

Angela S. Krebs
Michigan State University

James M. Larson
Michigan State University

Ronald Preston
Indiana University

Tat Ming Sze
Michigan State University

Sarah Theule-Lubienski
Michigan State University

Jeffrey J. Wanko
Michigan State University

Field Test Production Team

Katherine Oesterle
Michigan State University

Stacey L. Otto
University of North Carolina at Chapel Hill

Teacher/Assessment Team

Kathy Booth
Waverly, Michigan

Anita Clark
Marshall, Michigan

Theodore Gardella
Bloomfield Hills, Michigan

Yvonne Grant
Portland, Michigan

Linda R. Lobue
Vista, California

Suzanne McGrath
Chula Vista, California

Nancy McIntyre
Troy, Michigan

Linda Walker
Tallahassee, Florida

Software Developer

Richard Burgis
East Lansing, Michigan

Development Center Directors

Nicholas Branca
San Diego State University

Dianne Briars
Pittsburgh Public Schools

Frances R. Curcio
New York University

Perry Lanier
Michigan State University

J. Michael Shaughnessy
Portland State University

Charles Vonder Embse
Central Michigan University

Field Test Coordinators

Michelle Bohan
Queens, New York

Melanie Branca
San Diego, California

Alecia Devantier
Shepherd, Michigan

Jenny Jorgensen
Flint, Michigan

Sandra Kralovec
Portland, Oregon

Sonia Marsalis
Flint, Michigan

William Schaeffer
Pittsburgh, Pennsylvania

Karma Vince
Toledo, Ohio

Virginia Wolf
Pittsburgh, Pennsylvania

Shirel Yaloz
Queens, New York

Student Assistants

Laura Hammond
David Roche
Courtney Stoner
Jovan Trpovski
Julie Valicenti
Michigan State University

Advisory Board

Joseph Adney
Michigan State University (Emeritus)

Charles Allan
Michigan Department of Education

Mary K. Bouck
Portland Public Schools
Portland, Michigan

C. Stuart Brewster
Palo Alto, California

Anita Clark
Marshall Public Schools
Marshall, Michigan

David Doherty
GMI Engineering and Management Institute
Flint, Michigan

Kay Gilliland
EQUALS
Berkeley, California

David Green
GMI Engineering and Management Institute
Flint, Michigan

Henry Heikkinen
University of Northern Colorado
Greeley, Colorado

Anita Johnston
Jackson Community College
Jackson, Michigan

Elizabeth M. Jones
Lansing School District
Lansing, Michigan

Jim Landwehr
AT&T Bell Laboratories
Murray Hill, New Jersey

Peter Lappan
Michigan State University

Steven Leinwand
Connecticut Department of Education

Nancy McIntyre
Troy Public Schools
Troy, Michigan

Valerie Mills
Ypsilanti Public Schools
Ypsilanti, Michigan

David S. Moore
Purdue University
West Lafayette, Indiana

Ralph Oliva
Texas Instruments
Dallas, Texas

Richard Phillips
Michigan State University

Jacob Plotkin
Michigan State University

Dawn Pysarchik
Michigan State University

Rheta N. Rubenstein
University of Windsor
Windsor, Ontario, Canada

Susan Jo Russell
TERC
Cambridge, Massachusetts

Marjorie Senechal
Smith College
Northampton, Massachusetts

Sharon Senk
Michigan State University

Jacqueline Stewart
Okemos School District
Okemos, Michigan

Uri Treisman
University of Texas
Austin, Texas

Irvin E. Vance
Michigan State University

Linda Walker
Tallahassee Public Schools
Tallahassee, Florida

Gail Weeks
Northville Public Schools
Northville, Michigan

Pilot Teachers

California

National City

Laura Chavez
National City Middle School

Ruth Ann Duncan
National City Middle School

Sonia Nolla
National City Middle School

San Diego

James Ciolli
Los Altos Elementary School

Chula Vista

Agatha Graney
Hilltop Middle School

Suzanne McGrath
Eastlake Elementary School

Toni Miller
Hilltop Middle School

Lakeside

Eva Hollister
Tierra del Sol Middle School

Vista

Linda LoBue
Washington Middle School

Illinois

Evanston

Marlene Robinson
Baker Demonstration School

Michigan

Bloomfield Hills

Roxanne Cleveland
Bloomfield Hills Middle School

Constance Kelly
Bloomfield Hills Middle School

Tim Loula
Bloomfield Hills Middle School

Audrey Marsalese
Bloomfield Hills Middle School

Kara Reid
Bloomfield Hills Middle School

Joann Schultz
Bloomfield Hills Middle School

Flint

Joshua Coty
Holmes Middle School

Brenda Duckett-Jones
Brownell Elementary School

Lisa Earl
Holmes Middle School

Anne Heidel
Holmes Middle School

Chad Meyers
Brownell Elementary School

Greg Mickelson
Holmes Middle School

Rebecca Ray
Holmes Middle School

Patricia Wagner
Holmes Middle School

Greg Williams
Gundry Elementary School

Lansing

Susan Bissonette
Waverly Middle School

Kathy Booth
Waverly East Intermediate School

Carole Campbell
Waverly East Intermediate School

Gary Gillespie
Waverly East Intermediate School

Denise Kehren
Waverly Middle School

Virginia Larson
Waverly East Intermediate School

Kelly Martin
Waverly Middle School

Laurie Metevier
Waverly East Intermediate School

Craig Paksi
Waverly East Intermediate School

Tony Pecoraro
Waverly Middle School

Helene Rewa
Waverly East Intermediate School

Arnold Sticfcl
Waverly Middle School

Portland

Bill Carlton
Portland Middle School

Kathy Dole
Portland Middle School

Debby Flate
Portland Middle School

Yvonne Grant
Portland Middle School

Terry Keusch
Portland Middle School

John Manzini
Portland Middle School

Mary Parker
Portland Middle School

Scott Sandborn
Portland Middle School

Shepherd

Steve Brant
Shepherd Middle School

Marty Brock
Shepherd Middle School

Cathy Church
Shepherd Middle School

Ginny Crandall
Shepherd Middle School

Craig Ericksen
Shepherd Middle School

Natalie Hackney
Shepherd Middle School

Bill Hamilton
Shepherd Middle School

Julie Salisbury
Shepherd Middle School

Sturgis

Sandra Allen
Eastwood Elementary School

Margaret Baker
Eastwood Elementary School

Steven Baker
Eastwood Elementary School

Keith Barnes
Sturgis Middle School

Wilodean Beckwith
Eastwood Elementary School

Darcy Bird
Eastwood Elementary School

Bill Dickey
Sturgis Middle School

Ellen Eisele
Sturgis Middle School

James Hoelscher
Sturgis Middle School

Richard Nolan
Sturgis Middle School

J. Hunter Raiford
Sturgis Middle School

Cindy Sprowl
Eastwood Elementary School

Leslie Stewart
Eastwood Elementary School

Connie Sutton
Eastwood Elementary School

Traverse City

Maureen Bauer
Interlochen Elementary School

Ivanka Berskshire
East Junior High School

Sarah Boehm
Courtade Elementary School

Marilyn Conklin
Interlochen Elementary School

Nancy Crandall
Blair Elementary School

Fran Cullen
Courtade Elementary School

Eric Dreier
Old Mission Elementary School

Lisa Dzierwa
Cherry Knoll Elementary School

Ray Fouch
West Junior High School

Ed Hargis
Willow Hill Elementary School

Richard Henry
West Junior High School

Dessie Hughes
Cherry Knoll Elementary School

Ruthanne Kladder
Oak Park Elementary School

Bonnie Knapp
West Junior High School

Sue Laisure
Sabin Elementary School

Stan Malaski
Oak Park Elementary School

Jody Meyers
Sabin Elementary School

Marsha Myles
East Junior High School

Mary Beth O'Neil
Traverse Heights Elementary School

Jan Palkowski
East Junior High School

Karen Richardson
Old Mission Elementary School

Kristin Sak
Bertha Vos Elementary School

Mary Beth Schmitt
East Junior High School

Mike Schrotenboer
Norris Elementary School

Gail Smith
Willow Hill Elementary School

Karrie Tufts
Eastern Elementary School

Mike Wilson
East Junior High School

Tom Wilson
West Junior High School

Minnesota

Minneapolis

Betsy Ford
Northeast Middle School

New York

East Elmhurst

Allison Clark
Louis Armstrong Middle School

Dorothy Hershey
Louis Armstrong Middle School

J. Lewis McNeece
Louis Armstrong Middle School

Rossana Perez
Louis Armstrong Middle School

Merna Porter
Louis Armstrong Middle School

Marie Turini
Louis Armstrong Middle School

North Carolina

Durham

Everly Broadway
Durham Public Schools

Thomas Carson
Duke School for Children

Mary Hebrank
Duke School for Children

Bill O'Connor
Duke School for Children

Ruth Pershing
Duke School for Children

Peter Reichert
Duke School for Children

Elizabeth City

Rita Banks
Elizabeth City Middle School

Beth Chaundry
Elizabeth City Middle School

Amy Cuthbertson
Elizabeth City Middle School

Deni Dennison
Elizabeth City Middle School

Jean Gray
Elizabeth City Middle School

John McMenamin
Elizabeth City Middle School

Nicollette Nixon
Elizabeth City Middle School

Malinda Norfleet
Elizabeth City Middle School

Joyce O'Neal
Elizabeth City Middle School

Clevie Sawyer
Elizabeth City Middle School

Juanita Shannon
Elizabeth City Middle School

Terry Thorne
Elizabeth City Middle School

Rebecca Wardour
Elizabeth City Middle School

Leora Winslow
Elizabeth City Middle School

Franklinton

Susan Haywood
Franklinton Elementary School

Clyde Melton
Franklinton Elementary School

Louisburg

Lisa Anderson
Terrell Lane Middle School

Jackie Frazier
Terrell Lane Middle School

Pam Harris
Terrell Lane Middle School

Ohio

Toledo

Bonnie Bias
Hawkins Elementary School

Marsha Jackish
Hawkins Elementary School

Lee Jagodzinski
DeVeaux Junior High School

Norma J. King
Old Orchard Elementary School

Margaret McCready
Old Orchard Elementary School

Carmella Morton
DeVeaux Junior High School

Karen C. Rohrs
Hawkins Elementary School

Marie Sahloff
DeVeaux Junior High School

L. Michael Vince
McTigue Junior High School

Brenda D. Watkins
Old Orchard Elementary School

Oregon

Portland

Roberta Cohen
Catlin Gabel School

David Ellenberg
Catlin Gabel School

Sara Normington
Catlin Gabel School

Karen Scholte-Arce
Catlin Gabel School

West Linn

Marge Burack
Wood Middle School

Tracy Wygant
Athey Creek Middle School

Canby

Sandra Kralovec
Ackerman Middle School

Pennsylvania

Pittsburgh

Sheryl Adams
Reizenstein Middle School

Sue Barie
Frick International Studies Academy

Suzie Berry
Frick International Studies Academy

Richard Delgrosso
Frick International Studies Academy

Janet Falkowski
Frick International Studies Academy

Joanne George
Reizenstein Middle School

Harriet Hopper
Reizenstein Middle School

Chuck Jessen
Reizenstein Middle School

Ken Labuskes
Reizenstein Middle School

Barbara Lewis
Reizenstein Middle School

Sharon Mihalich
Reizenstein Middle School

Marianne O'Connor
Frick International Studies Academy

Mark Sammartino
Reizenstein Middle School

Washington

Seattle

Chris Johnson
University Preparatory Academy

Rick Purn
University Preparatory Academy

Contents

Throughout history we find records of the importance of measurement. In fact, in the early development of mathematics, geometry was synonymous with measurement. Today we are surrounded with ever-increasingly complex measures such as information-access rates, signal strength, and memory capacity.

The overarching goal of this unit is to help students begin to understand what it means to measure. Students study two kinds of measurements that are appropriate for grade 6: perimeter and area. Since students often have misconceptions about the effects of each of these measures on the other, it is critical to study them together and to probe their relationships. The problems in this unit are structured so that students can build a deep understanding of what it means to measure area and what it means to measure perimeter. In the process, they develop strategies for measuring perimeter and area of both rectangular and nonrectangular shapes.

The name of this unit indicates the theme that binds the investigations together: *covering* (area) and *surrounding* (perimeter). A subtheme running through the unit focuses on questions of what is the largest and what is the smallest, a precursor to the notions of maxima and minima. You will recognize connections throughout the *Covering and Surrounding* unit to all the units preceding it in the grade 6 curriculum. The connections to factors and multiples and to data gathering, organizing, and representing are especially strong.

The problems present interesting and challenging tasks while offering opportunities for meaningful progress and learning by students of different aptitudes and prior achievements. The student edition strongly supports investigative classwork. The greatest learning will occur if students conduct some exploratory work on their own, discover strategies for themselves, and then share their findings.

While this unit does not explicitly focus on the more global aspects of what it means to measure, it does lay the groundwork for teachers to raise issues that help students begin to see relationships and characteristics of all measurements.

The Measurement Process

The measurement process involves several key elements.

- *A phenomenon or object is chosen, and an attribute that can be measured is identified.* This could involve such disparate properties as height, mass, time, temperature, and capacity.

- *An appropriate unit is selected.* The unit depends on the kind of measure to be made and the degree of precision needed for the measure. Units of measurement include centimeters, angstroms, degrees, minutes, volts, and decibels; instruments for measuring include rulers, calipers, scales, watches, ammeters, springs, and weights.

- *The unit is used repeatedly to "match" the attribute of the phenomenon or object in an appropriate way.* This matching might be accomplished, for example, by "covering," "reaching the end of," "surrounding," or "filling" the object.

- *The number of units is determined.* The number of units is the measure of the property of the phenomenon or object.

Measuring Perimeter and Area

Covering and Surrounding highlights two important kinds of measures—perimeter and area—that depend on very different units and measurement processes. Measuring perimeter requires *linear* units; measuring area requires *square* units. Students often confuse these, and a strong emphasis on formulas may contribute to their confusion. While students can become adept at plugging numbers into formulas, they often have a hard time remembering which formula does what. This is often because they have an incomplete fundamental understanding of what the measurement is about.

Many students think that area and perimeter are related in that one determines the other. They may think that all rectangles of a given area have the same perimeter or that all rectangles of a given perimeter have the same area. The investigations in *Covering and Surrounding* help students realize for themselves the inaccuracy of such notions.

Covering and Surrounding takes an experimental approach to developing students' understanding of measuring perimeter and area. It is assumed that students will work with tiles, transparent grids, grid paper, string, rulers, and other devices of their choice to develop a dynamic sense of "covering" and "surrounding" to find area and perimeter. Many students who engage in these kinds of investigations do invent formulas for finding area and perimeter in certain situations. This should be encouraged, but not forced. Some students need the help of a more hands-on approach to measuring for quite a while. The payoff for allowing students the time and opportunity to develop levels of abstraction with which they are comfortable is that they will eventually make sense of perimeter and area in a lasting way.

Accuracy and Error

Measuring objects and comparing data from the whole class is an excellent way to help students begin to see that all measures are approximate. One can fine-tune measurements to get a degree of precision in a particular situation, but no matter how precise the instruments with which a measurement is made, error will always exist.

The investigations in *Covering and Surrounding* primarily involve whole-number situations. However, students will often approximate areas and perimeters and are likely to need fractions or decimals when measuring real objects. Students—especially those uncomfortable with fractions or decimals—may try to round all measurements to whole numbers. You will need to encourage them to use fractions or decimals so that their measurements are more accurate.

The notions of scale are fundamental to proportional reasoning. Because proportional reasoning is a key concept for the middle grades, it is important that students encounter many situations that call for reasoning about proportions. The familiarity of the situation can help students make sense of the relationships. Because they will be working with drawings that represent real objects, students will encounter problems of scale. We have tried to keep these problems manageable by carefully selecting scales that make for easy transitions from the model to the real object.

The investigations have a mix of metric and standard measures, with the metric system being used most of the time.

Terminology

Students will frequently encounter the terms *organize, explain, compare,* and *estimate* in this unit.

Asking students to organize their data means to display the data in a way that is convenient and useful for solving problems or finding patterns, as in a table.

Asking students to explain their solutions is intended to help them discover for themselves what they know and what they still need to find out—a student may have obtained an answer, but why does the answer make sense? Students will have opportunities to use a variety of representations to help them explain their solutions. In the process, students must share their thinking, a useful assessment for both student and teacher.

Students will often be asked to estimate or to compare measurements. Comparing and estimating are important skills used with many kinds of quantities, and they will help students develop skills in knowing whether an estimate is reasonable or appropriate, how to make estimates, and how to compare measurements in meaningful ways.

Covering *and Surrounding* was created to help students

- Develop strategies for finding areas and perimeters of rectangular shapes and then of nonrectangular shapes

- Discover relationships between perimeter and area

- Understand how the area of a rectangle is related to the area of a triangle and of a parallelogram

- Develop formulas or procedures—stated in words or symbols—for finding areas and perimeters of rectangles, parallelograms, triangles, and circles

- Use area and perimeter to solve applied problems

- Recognize situations in which measuring perimeter or area will answer practical problems

- Find perimeters and areas of rectangular and nonrectangular figures by using transparent grids, tiles, or other objects to cover the figures and string, straight-line segments, rulers, or other objects to surround the figures

- Cut and rearrange figures—in particular, parallelograms, triangles, and rectangles—to see relationships between them and then devise strategies for finding areas by using the observed relationships

- Observe and reason from patterns in data by organizing tables to represent the data

- Reason to find, confirm, and use relationships involving area and perimeter

- Use multiple representations—in particular, physical, pictorial, tabular, and symbolic models—and verbal descriptions of data

The overall goal of Connected Mathematics is to help students develop sound mathematical habits. Through their work in this and other geometry units, students learn important questions to ask themselves about any situation that can be represented and modeled mathematically, such as: *What properties of square tiles and rectangular tiles make them so useful for covering flat surfaces? How are the perimeter and area of a figure related? How can we find the perimeter of an irregular figure? How can we find the area? Can a figure have a small area but a large perimeter? Can a figure have a large area but a small perimeter? Are there special relationships between perimeter and area for 4-sided figures such as parallelograms? Is there a relationship between perimeter and area for triangles? Does a circle have perimeter and area? If so, how can they be found?*

Investigation 1: Measuring Perimeter and Area

Students build a good understanding of the difference between perimeter and area by dealing with the concepts concurrently in a concrete, manipulative setting. They use square tiles to create designs and to cover pictures of designs to find areas and perimeters, and they transform designs to fit a prescribed perimeter or area.

Investigation 2: Measuring Odd Shapes

Students consider the measuring of things with curved or irregular edges that can't be laid along a ruler. This calls for using other tools, such as string, to help find an approximation. They trace their feet on grid paper, estimate the perimeters and areas of the tracings, and discuss how these measurements might be helpful to shoe manufacturers.

Investigation 3: Constant Area, Changing Perimeter

This investigation introduces a classic maxima/minima problem, asking students to find the largest and the smallest perimeter for a given area. Students construct tables to help highlight and reveal patterns in data.

Investigation 4: Constant Perimeter, Changing Area

This investigation also focuses on maxima/minima questions, but this time perimeter is fixed and area is allowed to change. Students confront the misconception that area determines perimeter and vice versa.

Investigation 5: Measuring Parallelograms

Students cut and rearrange parallelograms to make rectangles and develop strategies for using what they know about finding the area of a rectangle to find the area of a parallelogram. Most students will develop good formulas for finding the area of a rectangle and a parallelogram. For students who need them, the use of grids and other more informal reasoning methods are encouraged.

Investigation 6: Measuring Triangles

Students are introduced to finding areas and perimeters of triangles by using grids, arranging triangles to form parallelograms, and measuring with rulers. Special triangles—such as isosceles and 30–60–90 triangles—are explored.

Investigation 7: Going Around in Circles

Questions are asked to help students see that the circumference (that is, the perimeter) of a circle is slightly more than three times its diameter, and that a circle's area is slightly more than three times the area of a square whose edges are equal to the circle's radius. These discoveries lead students to the idea of the value of pi.

Connections to Other Units

The ideas in *Covering and Surrounding* build on and connect to several big ideas in other Connected Mathematics units.

Big Idea	Prior Work	Future Work
interpreting area as the number of square units needed to cover a 2-D shape	creating tessellations (*Shapes and Designs*)	studying relationships between 3-D models and 2-D representations of the models (*Ruins of Montarek*); comparing areas of 2-D shapes to test for similarity (*Stretching and Shrinking*); finding surface area and volume of 3-D figures (*Filling and Wrapping*)
interpreting perimeter as the number of (linear) units needed to surround a 2-D shape	using Logo to construct shapes with the computer (*Shapes and Designs*)	studying relationship between 3-D models and 2-D representations of the models (*Ruins of Montarek*); looking at dimensions of similar figures to find scale factors (*Stretching and Shrinking*); finding surface area and volume of 3-D figures (*Filling and Wrapping*)
developing strategies for finding the perimeter and area of irregular 2-D shapes	performing operations with rational numbers; estimating sums of rational numbers (*Prime Time, Bits and Pieces I*)	developing strategies for estimating the surface area and volume of irregular 3-D figures (*Filling and Wrapping*)
studying the relationship between perimeter and area in rectangles	performing operations with whole numbers and finding factor pairs of whole numbers (*Prime Time*); using and constructing graphs on coordinate grids (*Data About Us*)	studying the relationship between the dimensions and volume of a prism (*Filling and Wrapping*)
developing strategies and algorithms for finding the perimeter and area of rectangles, triangles, parallelograms, and circles	subdividing and comparing shapes (*Shapes and Designs*); collecting data and looking for and generalizing patterns (*Prime Time, Shapes and Designs*)	developing strategies and algorithms for finding the surface area and volume of prisms, cones, and spheres (*Filling and Wrapping*)

Materials

For students

- Labsheets
- Calculators
- Grid paper in a variety of sizes (half-centimeter, centimeter, quarter-inch, half-inch, and inch grid paper are provided as blackline masters)
- Transparent centimeter and half-centimeter grids (a half-page grid of each size per student; copy the grids onto transparency film)
- Square tiles (about 24 per student, in a resealable package)
- Compasses
- Scissors
- Rulers
- String
- Tape measures
- Several circular objects
- Glue or tape
- Construction paper

For the teacher

- Transparencies and transparency markers (optional)
- Grid paper
- Transparencies of grid paper (optional; copy grids onto transparency film)

Technology

We expect that students will use calculators freely to perform arithmetic computations so that their focus can be on analyzing the problems and searching for patterns. Connected Mathematics was developed with the belief that calculators should always be available and that students should decide when to use them. For this reason, we do not designate specific problems as "calculator problems."

Pacing Chart

This pacing chart gives estimates of the class time required for each investigation and assessment piece. Shaded rows indicate opportunities for assessment.

Investigations and Assessments	Class Time
1 Measuring Perimeter and Area	4 days
2 Measuring Odd Shapes	2 days
3 Constant Area, Changing Perimeter	2 days
4 Constant Perimeter, Changing Area	2 days
Check-Up 1	1/2 day
Quiz A	1 day
5 Measuring Parallelograms	2 days
6 Measuring Triangles	4 days
7 Going Around in Circles	6 days
Check-Up 2	1/2 day
Quiz B	1 day
Self-Assessment	Take home
The Unit Test	1 day
The Unit Project	Take home

Vocabulary

The following words and concepts are introduced and used in *Covering and Surrounding*. Concepts in the left column are essential for student understanding of this and future units. The Descriptive Glossary describes many of these and other words used in *Covering and Surrounding*.

Essential	Nonessential
area	base
center (of a circle)	height
circle	length
circumference	width
diameter	pentomino
perimeter	perpendicular
radius (radii)	trapezoid
pi or π	

Assessment Summary

Embedded Assessment

Opportunities for informal assessment of student progress are embedded throughout *Covering and Surrounding* in the problems, the ACE questions, and the Mathematical Reflections. Suggestions for observing as students explore and discover mathematical ideas, for probing to guide their progress in developing concepts and skills, and for questioning to determine their level of understanding can be found in the *Launch, Explore,* or *Summarize* sections of all investigation problems. Some examples:

- Investigation 4, Problem 4.1 *Launch* (page 45a) suggests ways you can help your students understand the concept of holding the perimeter fixed, while letting the area vary.
- Investigation 5, Problem 5.2 *Explore* (page 55c) suggests questions you might ask students who finish the problem early.
- Investigation 2, Problem 2.1 *Summarize* (page 28a) suggests questions you might ask to assess your students' strategies for measuring irregular shapes.

ACE Assignments

An ACE (Applications—Connections—Extensions) section appears at the end of each investigation. To help you assign ACE questions, a list of assignment choices is given in the margin next to the reduced student page for each problem. Each list indicates the ACE questions that students should be able to answer after they complete the problem.

Partner Quizzes

Two quizzes, which may be given after Investigations 4 and 7, are provided with *Covering and Surrounding.* These quizzes are designed to be completed by pairs of students with the opportunity for revision based on teacher feedback. You will find the quizzes and their answer keys in the Assessment Resources section. As an alternative to the quizzes provided, you can construct your own quizzes by combining questions from the Question Bank, the quizzes, and unassigned ACE questions.

Check-Ups

Two check-ups, which may be given after Investigations 4 and 7, are provided for use as quick quizzes or warm-up activities. Check-ups are designed for students to complete individually. You will find the check-ups and their answer keys in the Assessment Resources section.

Question Bank

A Question Bank provides questions you can use for homework, reviews, or quizzes. You will find the Question Bank and its answer key in the Assessment Resources section.

Notebook/Journal

Students should have notebooks to record and organize their work. In the notebooks will be their journals along with sections for vocabulary, homework, and quizzes and check-ups. In their journals, students can take notes, solve investigation problems, write down ideas for their projects, and record their mathematical reflections. You should assess student journals for completeness rather than correctness; journals should be seen as "safe" places where students can try out their thinking. A Notebook Checklist and a Self-Assessment are provided in the Assessment Resources section. The Notebook Checklist helps students organize their notebooks. The Self-Assessment guides students as they review their notebooks to determine which ideas they have mastered and which ideas they still need to work on.

The Unit Project: Plan a Park

As a final assessment in *Covering and Surrounding*, you may administer the Unit Test or assign the Unit Project, Plan a Park. The project is introduced at the beginning of the unit, where students learn of a piece of land for which they will design a park. As students complete the investigations, they are asked to write about things they are learning that will help them to design the park. The project is formally assigned at the end of the unit, when students are asked to use what they have learned about perimeter and area to design and lay out their park. The project could be assigned to individuals, pairs, or small groups. A scoring rubric and a sample of student work are given in the Assessment Resources section.

The Unit Test

As final assessment in *Covering and Surrounding*, you may assign the Unit Project or administer the Unit Test. The Unit Test focuses on perimeters and areas of rectangles, triangles, and circles, and on the relationships between perimeter and area.

Introducing Your Students to *Covering and Surrounding*

Discuss the questions posed on the opening page of the student edition, which are designed to start students thinking about the kinds of questions and mathematics in the unit. Don't look for "correct" answers at this time. Do, however, present an opportunity for the class to discuss the questions and to start to think about units of measure and what kinds of measures are needed to answer the questions. You may want to revisit these questions as students learn mathematical ideas and techniques that will help them to answer such questions.

Covering and Surrounding

Pizza parlors often describe their selections as 9-inch, 12-inch, 15-inch, or even 24-inch pizzas. What do these measurements tell you about pizza size? How does the size of a pizza relate to its price? Does a 24-inch pizza generally cost twice as much as a 12-inch pizza? Should price relate to size in that way?

You may know that China has the greatest population of any country. Which country do you think has the greatest land area? The longest borders? Which state in the United States is the largest? Which state is the smallest? How do you think land area, borders, and coastlines of states and countries are measured?

Carpet is commonly sold by the square yard. How would you estimate the cost of carpet for a room in your home? Base molding, which is used to protect the bases of walls, is usually sold by the foot. How would you estimate the cost of base molding for a room in your home?

You can describe the size of something in lots of different ways. You can use words—such as *long, short, thin, wide, high,* and *low*—to give a general description of size. When you want to be more specific, you can use *numbers* and *units of measurement*—for example, centimeters, inches, and square feet.

The question on the opposite page all involve size. In this unit, you will learn mathematical ideas and techniques that can help you answer questions like these.

Mathematical Highlights

The Mathematical Highlights page provides information to students and to parents and other family members. It gives students a preview of the activities and problems in *Covering and Surrounding*. As they work through the unit, students can refer back to the Mathematical Highlights page to review what they have learned and to preview what is still to come. This page also tells students' families what mathematical ideas and activities will be covered as the class works through *Covering and Surrounding*.

Mathematical Highlights

In *Covering and Surrounding*, you will learn about area and perimeter.

● Designing and comparing floor plans for bumper-car rides helps you understand perimeter and area.

● Tracing and measuring your foot helps you develop ways to reason about the perimeter and area of odd shapes.

● Designing different storm shelters with the same area illustrates how perimeters of figures with the same area can vary.

● Investigating the different dog pens you can build with a fixed amount of fencing shows you how the areas of figures with the same perimeter can vary.

● Measuring parallelograms drawn on grid paper, building parallelograms under constraints, and making a rectangle by cutting apart a parallelogram and reassembling it lead you to discover shortcuts for finding the area and perimeter of a parallelogram.

● Measuring triangles drawn on grid paper, building triangles under constraints, and making parallelograms from two copies of a triangle lead you to discover a shortcut for finding the area of a triangle.

● Finding areas and circumferences of pizzas and other circular objects helps you find patterns relating the radius and diameter to the area and the circumference.

● Covering a circle with "radius squares" leads you to discover the formula for the area of a circle.

Using a Calculator

In this unit, you will be able to use your calculator to find areas and perimeters of geometric figures. As you work on the Connected Mathematics units, you may decide whether to use a calculator to help you solve a problem.

Plan a Park

A local philanthropist, Dr. Doolittle, has just donated a piece of land to the city for a park. The plot of land is rectangular, and it measures 120 yards by 100 yards. Dr. Doolittle has also offered to donate money for construction of the park.

Dr. Doolittle wants the park to be a place that people of all ages would like to visit. She wants half of the park to be a picnic and playground area. She wants to leave the decision about what to do with the other half of the park area to someone else. She has decided to hold a design contest for the layout of the park.

Covering and Surrounding involves finding areas and perimeters of various figures and shapes. Dr. Doolittle's park design project will use the ideas you will study. After you finish the investigations in this unit, you will create a design for the park, including a scale drawing and a report that gives the dimensions of all the items you have included in your park.

As you work through each investigation, think about how you might use what you are learning to help you with your project. In particular, think about these things:

* How much space is needed for a swing set or a slide? You will need to measure one in a park or school yard near you so that your design is realistic.

* How big are tennis courts or basketball courts? You will need to find out their dimensions if you choose to put them into your park design.

* If you put in tennis courts or basketball courts, will you want a fence around them? You will need to answer this question to complete your design.

Tips for the Linguistically Diverse Classroom

Rebus Scenario The Rebus Scenario technique is described in detail in *Getting to Know Connected Mathematics*. This technique involves sketching rebuses on the chalkboard that correspond to key words in the story or information you present orally. Example: some key words and phrases for which you may need to draw rebuses while discussing the material on this page: *park* (swings, a slide, trees), *money* (a dollar bill), *construction* (a bulldozer), *all ages* (stick figures of a toddler, teenager, and grandparent), *shapes* (squares, circles, rectangles), *fence* (a fence).

Introducing the Unit Project

The final assessment for *Covering and Surrounding*, Plan a Park, is introduced on this page and formally assigned at the end of the unit. Students are told the story of a piece of land to be developed into a park, and about a contest for the design of the park.

You can set the context for the project by having a short discussion with the class about parks in the area and the common elements of parks. This conversation could be extended by asking students to brainstorm about what they would put in a park if they could design one and listing their suggestions on the board.

Throughout the unit, students are reminded to think about how the ideas they are learning might help them with their park design. They are encouraged to visit local parks to learn more about how parks are structured. At the end of the unit, students are asked to complete a design package, detailing and justifying their ideas for the layout of the park.

See pages 82 and 107 for information about assigning the project. To help you assess the projects, see page 108 of the Assessment Resources section. Here you will find a possible scoring rubric and a sample of a student project.

The Investigations

The teaching materials for each investigation consist of three parts: an overview, student pages with teaching outlines, and detailed notes for teaching the investigation.

The overview of each investigation includes brief descriptions of the problems, the mathematical and problem-solving goals of the investigation, and a list of necessary materials.

Essential information for teaching the investigation is provided in the margins around the student pages. The "At a Glance" overviews are brief outlines of the Launch, Explore, and Summarize phases of each problem for reference as you work with the class. To help you assign homework, a list of "Assignment Choices" is provided next to each problem. Wherever space permits, answers to problems, follow-ups, ACE questions, and Mathematical Reflections appear next to the appropriate student pages.

The Teaching the Investigation section follows the student pages and is the heart of the Connected Mathematics curriculum. This section describes in detail the Launch, Explore, and Summarize phases for each problem. It includes all the information needed for teaching, along with suggestions for what you might say at key points in the teaching. Use this section to prepare lessons and as a guide for teaching an investigation.

Assessment Resources

The Assessment Resources section contains blackline masters and answer keys for quizzes, check-ups, and the Question Bank. It also provides guidelines for assigning and assessing the unit project. A sample of student work, along with a teacher's comments about how the sample was assessed, will help you to evaluate your students' efforts. Blackline masters for the Notebook Checklist and the Self-Assessment are given. These instruments support student self-evaluation, an important aspect of assessment in the Connected Mathematics curriculum.

Blackline Masters

The Blackline Masters section includes masters for all labsheets and transparencies. Blackline masters of inch, quarter-inch, half-inch, centimeter, and half-centimeter grid paper are also provided.

Additional Practice

Practice pages for each investigation offer additional problems for students who need more practice with the basic concepts developed in the investigations as well as some continual review of earlier concepts.

Descriptive Glossary

The Descriptive Glossary provides descriptions and examples of the key concepts in *Covering and Surrounding*. These descriptions are not intended to be formal definitions, but are meant to give you an idea of how students might make sense of these important concepts.

Measuring Perimeter and Area

This investigation introduces students to area and perimeter by asking them to create floor plans for bumper-car rides made from 1-meter-square floor tiles and 1-meter rail sections. The floor tiles and rail sections allow students to count to find the area and perimeter of the plans. Counting is a natural and appropriate way for students to find area and perimeter, because measurement *is* counting. When we measure, we are *counting* the number of measurement units needed to "match" an attribute of an object.

This investigation builds firm ideas about what it means to measure area and perimeter and develops reasonably efficient strategies for finding area and perimeter. Mastery is not the goal at this point. Over time, students will become more efficient at measuring, but the ideas need time to settle in.

In Problem 1.1, students explore the different bumper-car floor plans that can be made from a given number of tiles. In Problem 1.2, students measure and compare three floor plans. In Problem 1.3, students compare the costs of building several different bumper-car floor plans. They find that, although designs may have the same area (number of floor tiles), the cost varies because the perimeters (number of rail sections) vary. The work with tiles in Problem 1.4 helps to solidify one of the main ideas of this investigation: figures with the same area may have different perimeters, and figures with the same perimeter may have different areas.

Mathematical and Problem-Solving Goals

- *To learn that the area of an object is the number of unit squares needed to cover it and the perimeter of an object is the number of units of length needed to surround it*

- *To understand that two figures with the same area may have different perimeters and that two figures with the same perimeter may have different areas*

- *To visualize what changes occur when tiles forming a figure are rearranged, added, or subtracted*

Materials		
Problem	**For students**	**For the teacher**
All	Calculators, centimeter grid paper (provided as a blackline master)	Transparencies 1.1 to 1.4 (optional)
1.1	Square tiles (24 per student)	Square tiles
1.2	Inch grid paper (provided as a blackline master) or one-inch tiles (about 20 per student)	
1.4	Square tiles (24 per student)	Blank transparencies (optional)

Designing Bumper-Car Rides

Grouping:
Pairs

Launch

- Introduce the bumper-car design problem by exploring simple designs as a class.

Explore

- Allow time for students to experiment with the tiles.

- As you circulate, verify that students' sketches clearly show 36 tiles.

Summarize

- Have pairs share their designs.

- Keep the class focused on the perimeters of the different designs.

- Talk about the need for always labeling measures of perimeter with the unit and measures of area with the square unit.

Assignment Choices

Ask students to think about and discuss with their families how covering and surrounding comes up in everyday experiences. Ask that students be prepared to share their conversations.

INVESTIGATION 1

Measuring Perimeter and Area

Most Americans enjoy the rides at amusement parks and carnivals—from merry-go-rounds and Ferris wheels to roller coasters and bumper cars.

Let's suppose that a company called Midway Amusement Rides—MARs for short—builds and operates a variety of rides for amusement parks and carnivals. To do well in their business, MARs has to apply some mathematical thinking.

1.1 Designing Bumper-Car Rides

MARs sells many of its rides to traveling shows that set up their carnivals in parking lots of shopping centers and in community parks. Because they must be easy to take apart and transport, rides for traveling shows must be smaller than rides found in large amusement parks.

Bumper cars are one of the most popular rides in traveling shows. A bumper-car ride includes the cars and a smooth floor with bumper rails around it. MARs makes their bumper-car floors from tiles that are 1 meter by 1 meter squares. The bumper rail is built from sections that are 1 meter long.

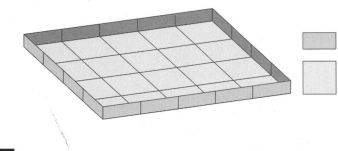

Bumper rail section

Floor tile (top view)

When MARs gets an order for a bumper-car ride, their designers sometimes use square tiles to model the possible floor plans, and then send sketches of their ideas to the customer for approval.

Problem 1.1

Solve these design problems by experimenting with square tiles.

A. Badger State Shows in Wisconsin requested a bumper-car ride with a total of 36 square meters of floor space and 26 rail sections. Sketch some possible designs for this floor plan.

B. Lone Star Carnivals in Texas wants a bumper-car ride that covers 36 square meters of floor space and has lots of rail sections for riders to bump against. Sketch some possible designs for this floor plan.

C. Design a bumper-car floor plan with 36 or more square meters of floor space that you think would make an interesting ride. Be prepared to share your design with the class and to explain why you like it.

▓ Problem 1.1 Follow-Up

Two measures tell you important facts about the size of the bumper-car floor plans you have designed. The number of tiles needed to *cover* the floor is the **area** of the shape. The number of bumper rail sections needed to *surround* the floor is the **perimeter** of the shape.

1. Find the perimeter and area of each bumper-car floor plan you designed in Problem 1.1.

2. Which measure—perimeter or area—better indicates the size of a bumper-car floor plan?

Answers to Problem 1.1

A. See page 18g.

B. See page 18g.

C. Answers will vary.

Answers to Problem 1.1 Follow-Up

1. The design for A has an area of 36 square meters and a perimeter of 26 meters. The perimeters of the designs for B will vary, but all should have an area of 36 square meters. Designs for part C will vary, but all should have an area of 36 square meters or larger.

2. Area is probably a better measure, because it indicates the amount of space available for the bumper cars.

Decoding Designs

Launch

- Make sure students understand the design problem.

Explore

- As students work on the problem, check that they are properly labeling their sketches.

Summarize

- Have students share their designs and their strategies for finding area and perimeter.

- If some students have calculated area using multiplication, allow them to share this strategy with the class.

Assignment Choices

ACE questions 1 and 6–9 (1 requires paper tiles)

1.2 Decoding Designs

The MARs company advertises its carnival rides in a catalog. One section of the catalog shows bumper-car floor plans. The catalog shows only outlines of the plans, not the grid of the floor tiles or the rail sections. Below are three of the designs shown in the catalog.

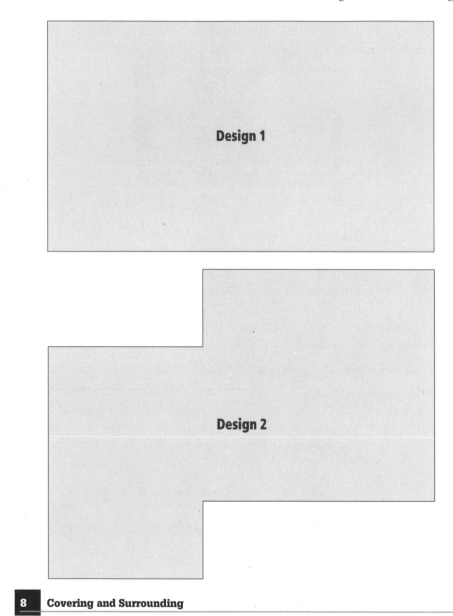

Design 1

Design 2

Design 3

Problem 1.2

Use the sample rail section and floor tile below to answer these questions.

A. Which of the three designs provides the greatest floor space (has the greatest area)?

B. Which of the three designs requires the most rail sections (has the greatest perimeter)?

Sample rail section   Sample floor tile section

▨ Problem 1.2 Follow-Up

Choose the design you think is best, and explain how you would sell it to a customer.

Answers to Problem 1.2

A. Design 3, with an area of 16 square units, provides the most floor space. Designs 1 and 2 each have an area of 15 square units.

B. Design 2, with a perimeter of 18 units, requires the greatest number of rail sections. Designs 1 and 3 each have a perimeter of 16 units.

Answers to Problem 1.2 Follow-Up

Possible answer: Design 3 is the best because it has more floor space than the other designs but uses the same number or fewer rails. Because of the larger space, you could put more cars on the floor at one time. This allows you to earn more money with each turn.

Computing Costs

At a Glance

Grouping:
Individuals or Pairs

Launch

- Introduce students to the problem.

- If students need help, work through design A as a class.

Explore

- As students work, make sure they are finding perimeter correctly.

Summarize

- Have students share the information from their tables.

- Ask questions to encourage students to notice relationships among area, perimeter, and cost.

- Make sure all students can use a counting strategy to find perimeter and area.

Assignment Choices

Unassigned choices from earlier problems

1.3 **Computing Costs**

The designers at MARs specialize in creating unusual floor plans for bumper-car rides. But when it comes time to prepare estimates or bills for customers, they turn the plans over to the billing department.

The Buckeye Amusements company in Ohio wants some sample designs and cost estimates for small bumper-car rides designed for children in small cars. The MARs designers came up with the floor plans below.

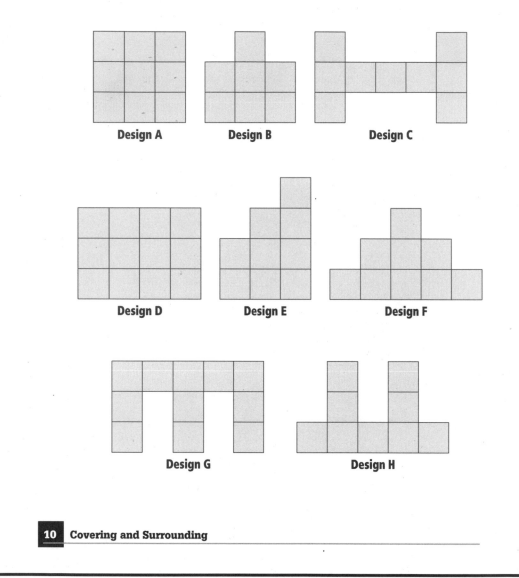

Design A   Design B   Design C

Design D   Design E   Design F

Design G   Design H

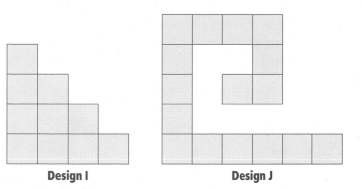

Design I   **Design J**

Problem 1.3

A. The MARs company charges $25 for each rail section and $30 for each floor tile. How much would each of the designs above cost? Record your data in a table with these column headings:

Design	Area	Perimeter	Cost of tiles	Cost of rail sections	Total cost

B. If you were the buyer for Buckeye Amusements, which design would you choose? Explain your choice.

■ **Problem 1.3 Follow-Up**

1. Of the designs above, which have an area of 9 square meters?

2. Give the price of each design you listed in question 1.

3. What accounts for the difference in the prices of the designs you listed in question 1?

Answers to Problem 1.3

A. See page 18g.

B. Answers will vary. Students should consider both price and design in their answers.

Answers to Problem 1.3 Follow-Up

1. designs A, C, E, F, and H

2. design A: $570, design C: $770, design E: $620, design F: $670, design H: $770

3. The designs have different perimeters. Larger perimeters require more rail section and, as a result, cost more to build.

1.4

Getting Your Money's Worth

Five of the bumper-car designs in Problem 1.3 had an area of 9 square meters. You found that these designs had different prices because their perimeters were different.

Questions A–E refer to the designs from Problem 1.3. Experiment with your tiles to try to answer the questions. Make sketches of your designs.

A. Build a design with the same area as design G, but with a smaller perimeter. Can you make more than one design that meets these requirements? Explain.

B. Design E can be made from design D by removing three tiles. How does the area of design D compare to the area of design E? How does the perimeter of design D compare to the perimeter of design E?

C. Design F and design I have the same perimeter. Can you rearrange the tiles of design F to make design I? Explain.

D. Design A and design C have the same area. Can you rearrange the tiles of design A to make design C? Explain.

E. Arrange your tiles to match design B. Now, move one tile to make a new design with a perimeter of 14 units. Sketch your new design.

■ Problem 1.4 Follow-Up

If two tile designs have the same area and the same perimeter, must they look exactly alike? Make a sketch to help explain your answer.

At a Glance

Grouping:
Pairs

Launch

■ Summarize Problem 1.3, making sure students know they will be again working with the designs from that problem.

Explore

■ As pairs finish, have them copy some of their designs for use in the summary.

Summarize

■ As a class, discuss the designs students found and the strategies they used for finding them.

■ Ask questions centering on the issue of how figures of the same area can be constructed with different perimeters.

Assignment Choices

ACE questions 2–5, 10, 11, 14–18 (2–5, 17, and 18 require grid paper and tiles or grid-paper squares; 11 requires grid paper), and unassigned choices from earlier problems

Answers to Problem 1.4

See page 18h.

Applications • Connections • Extensions

As you work on these ACE questions, use your calculator whenever you need it.

Applications

1. Cut out several 1-inch paper tiles. Cover this figure with your tiles. Record the area and the perimeter of the figure.

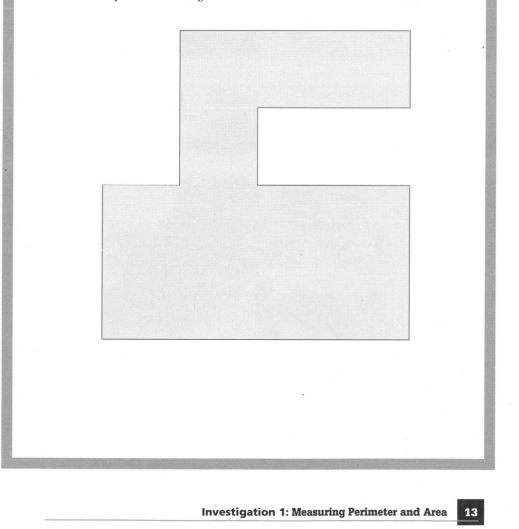

Investigation 1: Measuring Perimeter and Area **13**

Answers to Problem 1.4 Follow-Up

Having the same area and the same perimeter does not guarantee that two designs will be the same. For example, all of these figures have an area of 5 and a perimeter of 12:

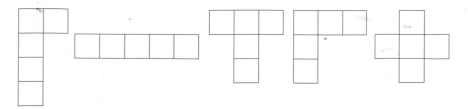

2. Possible answers:

3. Possible answers:

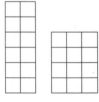

4. Possible answers:

5. Possible answers:

6. area = 6 square units, perimeter = 14 units

7. area = 20 square units, perimeter = 22 units

8. area = 26 square units, perimeter = 30 units

9. area = 20 square units, perimeter = 26 units

In 2–5, experiment with tiles or squares of grid paper. Sketch your final answers on grid paper.

2. Draw at least two shapes with an area of 6 square units and a perimeter of 12 units.

3. Draw at least two shapes with an area of 15 square units and a perimeter of 18 units.

4. Draw at least two shapes with an area of 12 square units and different perimeters.

5. Draw at least two shapes with a perimeter of 12 units and different areas.

In 6–9, find the area and perimeter of the shape.

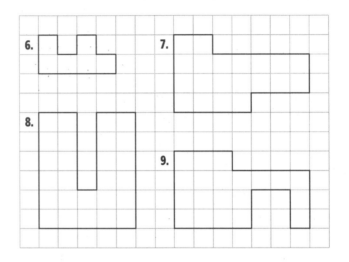

10. Look at this plan for design H.

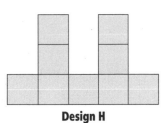

Design H

    a. If possible, design a figure with the same area as design H, but with a perimeter of 14 units. If this is not possible, explain why.

    b. If possible, design a figure with the same area as design H, but with a perimeter of 30 units. If this is not possible, explain why.

11.   **a.** Copy design J onto grid paper. Add six squares to make a new design with a perimeter of 22 units.

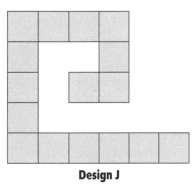

Design J

    b. Explain why the perimeters of your new design and design J are so different.

10a. Possible answer:

10b. See below left.

11a. See below left.

11b. When you fill in the inner parts of the spiral of design J with six squares, you get a 4×5 rectangle with a 2-square tail. Adding the squares on the inside eliminates many of the exposed edges in design J, giving it a much smaller perimeter. Design J is long and stringy; the new figure is more compact.

10b. Possible answer: It isn't possible to make a shape with perimeter 30 units using only 9 tiles. The largest perimeter you can get is by putting the squares in a straight line, which gives a perimeter of 20 units.

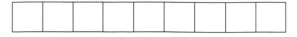

11a.

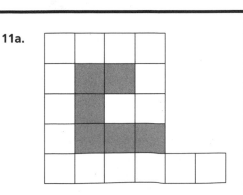

12a. Possible answer: You could draw two imaginary horizontal lines across the room, dividing the floor into three rectangles: one by the door, one in the nook by the window, and a large one taking up the majority of the floor's surface. You would then measure the length and width of each rectangle (in yards) and multiply the two measurements to find the areas (in square yards) of each rectangle. Add the areas together, and multiply the sum by the cost per square yard. A more likely answer: You could get a square that is 1 yard by 1 yard and lay it all over the room and see about how many it would take to cover it. You could take that number and multiply it by the cost for each square yard.

12b. Possible answer: You could lay a ruler all around the edge of the room, counting as you go. You would multiply the total by the cost per foot.

Connections

13. Possible answer: fd 20 rt 90 fd 80 rt 90 fd 20 rt 90 fd 80

14. See right.

15. See page 18i.

16. See page 18i.

---

12. Carpet is commonly sold by the square yard. Base molding is commonly sold by the foot.

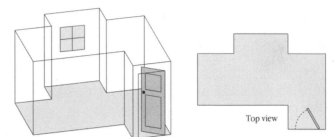

Top view

a. Describe a method you could use to *estimate* the cost of carpet for the room sketched here.

b. Describe a method you could use to *estimate* the cost of installing base molding around the base of the walls of this room.

Connections

13. Write a Logo program that will draw a rectangle with a perimeter of 200 turtle steps. Then, write a Logo program that will draw a *different* rectangle with a perimeter of 200 turtle steps.

You can describe the size and shape of a rectangle with just two numbers, *length* and *width*. In 14–16, sketch a rectangle on grid paper with the given area and with length and width that are whole numbers. Label each rectangle with its length and width.

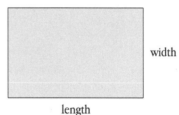

width

length

14. 18 square units

15. 20 square units

16. 23 square units

---

14. Possible answers:

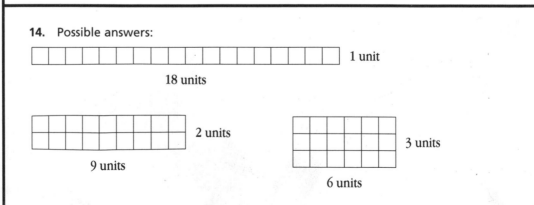

1 unit

18 units

2 units

9 units

3 units

6 units

Extensions

In 17 and 18, experiment with tiles or squares of grid paper, then sketch your answers on grid paper.

17. Draw at least two shapes with a perimeter of 18 units but with different areas. Give the area of each shape.

18. Draw at least two shapes with an area of 25 square units but with different perimeters. Give the perimeter of each shape.

19. The figures drawn on the grid below are not made up entirely of whole squares.

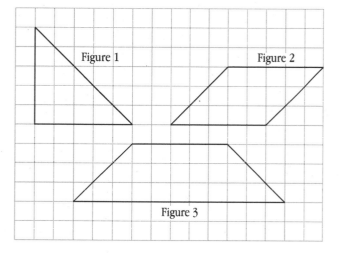

Figure 1

Figure 2

Figure 3

a. How would you find the area and perimeter of each figure?

b. For each figure, try your method, and record your estimates for area and perimeter.

Extensions

17. See page 18i.

18. See page 18i.

19a. See page 18j.

19b. Figure 1 (a triangle) has an area of 12.5 square units and a perimeter of about 17 units. Figure 2 (a parallelogram) has an area of 15 square units and a perimeter of about 18 units. Figure 3 (a trapezoid) has an area of 24 square units and a perimeter of about 24 units.

Mathematical Reflections

In this investigation, you examined the areas and perimeters of figures made from square tiles. You found that some arrangements of tiles have large perimeters and some arrangements have smaller perimeters. These questions will help you summarize what you have learned:

1 Is it possible for two shapes to have the same area but different perimeters? Explain your answer by using words and drawings.

2 Is it possible for two shapes to have the same perimeter but different areas? Explain your answer by using words and drawings.

3 Can you figure out the perimeter of a figure if you know its area? Why or why not?

Think about your answers to these questions, discuss your ideas with other students and your teacher, and then write a summary of your findings in your journal.

At the end of this unit, you will be designing the layout for a city park. Start thinking now about what things you should consider as you create your layout. How could you apply what you know about area and perimeter to your park design?

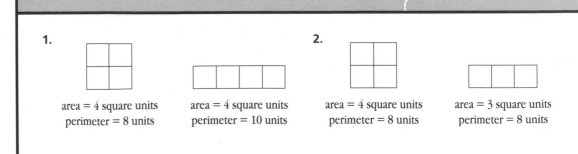

1.

area = 4 square units
perimeter = 8 units

area = 4 square units
perimeter = 10 units

2.

area = 4 square units
perimeter = 8 units

area = 3 square units
perimeter = 8 units

TEACHING THE INVESTIGATION

1.1 • Designing Bumper-Car Rides

In this problem, students are asked to design three bumper-car floor plans: one with an area of 36 square meters and a perimeter of 26 meters, a second with an area of 36 square meters and "many" rail sections, and a third with an area of 36 or more square meters. The follow-up questions introduce the terms *area* (for covering) and *perimeter* (for surrounding).

Launch

Launch the problem by telling students about the fictitious Midway Amusement Rides company. You might help your students with the context by adding to the story.

> These tiles are similar to what the designers use to make their models of bumper-car floor plans. (*Hold up a tile.*) Each tile represents 1 square meter.

> Let's think of this tile as the world's simplest bumper-car floor plan. A design that consists of only one tile represents a 1-square-meter design that would require 4 meters of bumper rail to surround it. Of course, this would only hold a very small car!

Begin a table on the board for recording data.

Number of tiles	Number of rails
1	4

> Now make a bumper-car floor plan from two tiles.

Make sure the class understands that the tiles of bumper-car floor plans must fit together edge to edge.

allowed   **not allowed**

> How many meters of railing would this floor need? (*6*)

> I notice that some of you have your tiles arranged this way. (*Hold up, or display on the overhead projector, the following arrangements.*)

And some of you have your tiles arranged this way.

Did you get the same number of rails for each of these arrangements?
(*Yes*)

Since the different orientations use the same number of tiles and the
same number of rails, we can list the information once (*Add 2 to the
"Number of tiles" column and 6 to the "Number of rails" column.*)

Number of tiles	Number of rails
1	4
2	6

Show me a design made of 3 square meters. How many meters of railing does it need?

Some of you have arranged your tiles this way. (*Show the following
arrangement.*)

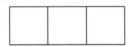

And some of you have arranged your tiles this way.

Do these two arrangements require the same number of rail sections?
(*Yes; add the information about three tiles to the chart.*)

Number of tiles	Number of rails
1	4
2	6
3	8

Show me a design with 4 square meters of flooring. How many meters
of railing does it need?

Here are some possible designs:

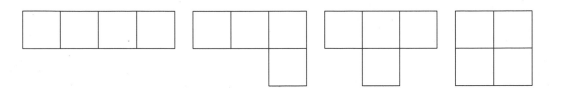

The first three designs require 10 meters of railing. The 2 × 2 design requires only 8 meters of railing. Record both possibilities on the chart:

Number of tiles	Number of rails
1	4
2	6
3	8
4	10
4	8

Ask students whether there are other numbers of tiles that can be arranged in more than one way so that different numbers of rail sections are required. Do not try to find a definite answer at this time: leave the question for students to think about.

If students are still struggling with constructing designs for a given number of tiles or figuring out how many rails are needed to surround a design, you may want to continue the exploration by asking students to design bumper-car floors with 12 tiles. Here are a few possible arrangements:

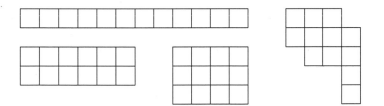

You would need 26 rail sections for the 1 × 12 rectangle, 16 for the 2 × 6 rectangle, 14 for the 3 × 4 rectangle, and 18 for the given shape that is not a rectangle.

Students should now be ready to tackle Problem 1.1. Have students make sketches of their designs on grid paper so that they can reuse their tiles for the next part of the problem. This is a good problem to be done in pairs.

Explore

Students will need time to talk about and experiment with the tiles. As you visit with them, be sure their sketches are complete and clearly show that 36 tiles have been used in each design.

Summarize

Have pairs share their results and explain why their designs meet the requirements. Keep students focused on the mathematics and what is happening to the perimeter—the number of rails needed—as they look at the variety of designs.

Discuss the ideas and questions presented in the follow-up. Talk about why measures of area should always be labeled with the square unit and measures of perimeter should always be labeled with the unit of length. Area is labeled in square units because it is a measurement of how many squares of a certain size are needed to *cover* a shape. Perimeter is labeled in units of length because it is a measurement of how many segments of a specific length are needed to *surround* a shape.

1.2 • Decoding Designs

This problem is a continuation of the ideas addressed in Problem 1.1. Many students will count to find area and perimeter, but some may use multiplication to find the areas of designs 1 and 3. You are not trying to develop a formula for the area of a rectangle at this point, but if some students are using it—and can explain why it makes sense—have them share their ideas.

Launch

Read through the problem with your class. The edges of the designs are whole numbers of inches. If you do not have one-inch tiles, you can pass out sheets of inch grid paper so students can cut out "paper tiles" and use them to cover the designs.

Explore

This short problem could easily be worked on by students individually. As you circulate, make sure students are finding the perimeter and area for each design.

Summarize

Have students report the perimeter and area for each design and describe their strategies for finding the measures. After each student gives his or her answers, ask the class whether they agree and whether they used a different strategy.

Design 3 is interesting because the area and perimeter both measure 16. In one class, a student suggested that *all* squares have the same number for area and perimeter. When several other students agreed, the teacher asked them to build squares of different sizes and find the perimeter

Side length	Area	Perimeter
1 unit	1 square unit	4 units
2 units	4 square units	8 units
3 units	9 square units	12 units
4 units	16 square units	16 units
5 units	25 square units	20 units

and area of each. The class made a chart of their data and quickly realized that the conjecture was false.

The teacher asked why it makes sense that these two measures would not be the same number and what was special about a square with sides of length 4 that makes the area and perimeter have the same measure.

She then asked whether students noticed anything else about the information in the chart. One student observed that perimeters are larger numbers than areas until the square of side length 4, for which they are equal; for squares with side lengths greater than 4, the perimeter is smaller than area. The teacher asked whether the next square's perimeter would be a smaller number than its area. Students built a square of side length 6 and found that it was. The teacher asked why the pattern was occurring. Students were unsure, so she suggested they continue to think about the question and that maybe they would find the answer after they had learned more about perimeter and area.

You may wish to handle unanswered questions such as these by posting the questions where they are clearly visible and returning to them occasionally for further discussion.

1.3 • Computing Costs

In this problem, students examine ten different floor plans. They continue to find perimeters and areas, but now they also look at the costs of building different designs. Some plans have the same area but different perimeters; others have the same perimeter but different areas. Students will calculate the cost for each design based on a per-unit cost.

Launch

Read through the problem with your class. If you think students are confused about what is being asked, work as a class to fill in the table for design A. Allow students to continue working on the problem, individually or in pairs.

Explore

As you observe students working, help those who are still confused about perimeter. Some may be counting the squares that line the edge of the figure instead of counting the edge lengths around the outside of the figure.

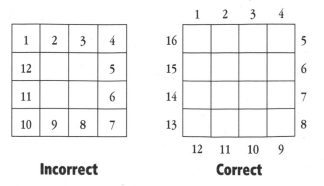

Incorrect   **Correct**

Summarize

Begin a conversation to get students to share the information in their charts and to encourage them to look for relationships among area, perimeter, and cost.

> What is the area of design A? Did any other designs have an area of 9 square meters? Did all these designs have the same perimeter? Which design with an area of 9 square meters had the smallest perimeter? Which design with an area of 9 square meters had the largest perimeter? How do the costs of these designs compare?

> What is the perimeter of design A? Did any other designs have a perimeter of 12 meters? Did all of these designs have the same area? How do the costs of the designs with a perimeter of 12 meters compare?

The discussion should emphasize that although many designs have the same area, the perimeter and cost vary. Similarly, many designs have the same perimeter, but varying area and cost.

Have students explain how they found area and perimeter. By asking these questions again, you can verify that students can at least find both measurements by counting. By this point in the unit, all students should be able to count squares to find area and count exposed edges to find perimeter. If some are still struggling, find a way for them to get additional help and practice with these concepts.

1.4 • Getting Your Money's Worth

This problem asks students to work with the designs from Problem 1.3, making adjustments in area or perimeter. In some cases several answers are possible; in others there is only one answer or the manipulation is impossible.

Launch

The summary of Problem 1.3 will serve to launch Problem 1.4. You may want to read the problem with your class to get them started. Make it clear that the designs being referred to are those from Problem 1.3. You may want students to record their results on grid paper. Whenever possible, students should record at least two designs and label the area and perimeter of each.

Explore

This problem is ideally done in pairs. However, all students should record the results for reference during the summary. If students are struggling, have them make their designs with tiles, manipulate the tiles to the desired results, and then record their results on grid paper.

Have pairs that finish early copy their solutions to one or more of the questions on a transparency or on the board to share. If pairs have different solutions to the same problem, have each record its results so the class can compare them.

Summarize

Discuss as many solutions to questions A–E as the class produced. For A, there are many arrangements with an area of 11 square meters and a perimeter of less than 24 meters. You could talk about the designs by grouping them by perimeter. Be sure students share the strategies they used to find the figures. Ask questions that encourage discussion of how the perimeter can be reduced without changing the area. A related issue also arises in question D; again, discuss the many solutions to the question.

Additional Answers

Answers to Problem 1.1

A. Answers will vary. Possible answers: The track could be a 4 × 9 rectangle, or a 5 × 7 rectangle with an additional square somewhere.

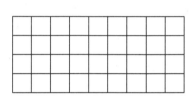

B. Possible answer:

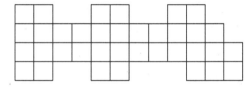

area = 36 square meters
perimeter = 40 meters

The largest perimeter possible for 36 squares is 74 meters, but it wouldn't make a very interesting bumper-car design:

Answers to Problem 1.3

A.

Design	Area	Perimeter	Cost of tiles	Cost of rail sections	Total cost
A	9 square meters	12 meters	$270	$300	$570
B	7 square meters	12 meters	$210	$300	$510
C	9 square meters	20 meters	$270	$500	$770
D	12 square meters	14 meters	$360	$350	$710
E	9 square meters	14 meters	$270	$350	$620
F	9 square meters	16 meters	$270	$400	$670
G	11 square meters	24 meters	$330	$600	$930
H	9 square meters	20 meters	$270	$500	$770
I	10 square meters	16 meters	$300	$400	$700
J	16 square meters	34 meters	$480	$850	$1330

Answers to Problem 1.4

A. Design G has an area of 11 square meters and a perimeter of 24 meters. Several figures can be constructed with an area of 11 square meters and a perimeter of less than 24 meters. Possible answers:

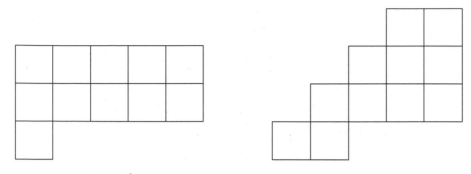

perimeter = 16 meters   perimeter = 18 meters

B. You can remove the shaded squares to get design E from design D. The area of design D (12 square meters) is three more than the area of design E (9 square meters). The perimeter of both designs is 14 meters.

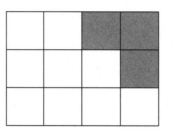

C. No, you cannot rearrange design F to get design I because they are made from different numbers of tiles. Design F has an area of 9 square meters and design I has an area of 10 square meters.

D. Yes, the figures are made from the same number of tiles, so you can rearrange the tiles in design A to make design C.

E. Possible solution: Move the shaded square as shown, producing a new figure of area 7 square meters but perimeter 14 meters.

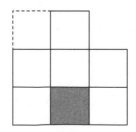

ACE Answers

Connections

15.

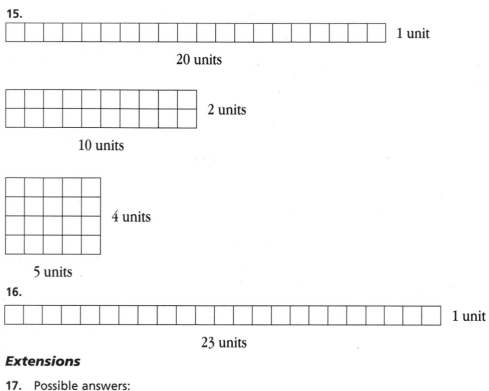

20 units

10 units

5 units

16.

1 unit

23 units

Extensions

17. Possible answers:

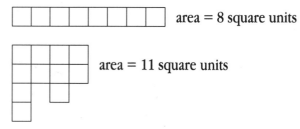

area = 8 square units

area = 11 square units

18. Possible answers:

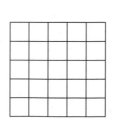

perimeter = 20 units   perimeter = 52 units

19a. Possible answer: For area, you could count all the whole squares and then put parts of other squares together to make a good estimate. For perimeter, you could first count the unit lengths for the sides that line up with the grid. For the sides that don't line up with the grid, you could mark each length on a strip of paper and then line the strip up with the grid to determine the length in grid units.

For the Teacher: Measuring Grids

These grids are marked off in quarter inches. When students estimate perimeter, they can use inch rulers and count every quarter inch as 1 unit.

Watch for students who count the diagonals of the small squares as 1 unit of length; this is a common mistake. Take time to discuss why that is incorrect by posing examples such as this:

If you walked across a baseball field from home plate to second base (at the opposite corner), would your walk be shorter or longer than the walk from home base to first base?

Measuring Odd Shapes

Students often first encounter area and perimeter through formulas for rectangles and other "nice" shapes. They may become facile at substituting numbers into formulas but miss developing an understanding of the underlying concepts. Investigation 1 focused on understanding and measuring area and perimeter in situations that can be modeled with tiles and grid paper. However, many things in the world for which we need to know area and perimeter cannot be covered with whole square units. This investigation looks at such figures—nongeometric shapes for which there are no formulas for finding area and perimeter.

The mathematical techniques used to estimate areas and perimeters of nongeometric shapes are powerful yet concrete. Finding areas of such shapes helps students to see the power of formulas to help solve some cases and the need to understand the underlying concepts so that techniques to solve more complex cases can be invented. The techniques of estimating the area and perimeter of nongeometric shapes are closely tied to the unit's title: *Covering and Surrounding*.

In Problem 2.1, Making the Shoe Fit, students find several measurements of their feet. Because their footprints cannot be covered with an exact number of squares, they must invent ways to estimate the measurements based on their understanding of area and perimeter.

Mathematical and Problem-Solving Goals

- *To understand the meaning of area and perimeter*

- *To develop techniques for estimating areas and perimeters of nongeometric figures*

- *To develop strategies for organizing and comparing data*

- *To use graphs to organize data and to make predictions*

Materials		
Problem	**For students**	**For the teacher**
All	Calculators, string, centimeter rulers, centimeter grid paper (provided as a blackline master)	Transparency 2.1 (optional), transparencies of centimeter and half-centimeter grid paper (optional; provided as a blackline master)

Student Pages   Teaching the Investigation

INVESTIGATION 2

Measuring Odd Shapes

It's not hard to find areas and perimeters of shapes made of complete squares. But measuring areas and perimeters of more interesting figures is not always easy.

2.1 Making the Shoe Fit

The clothes people wear come in many shapes and sizes. Shoes, for instance, are manufactured in thousands of types and styles. To make shoes that fit comfortably, shoe companies must know a lot about human feet.

In this problem, you will look at measures of feet and think about what measures a shoe company would need to know.

Did you know?

Although shoes are important to protect feet, for many people, they are also a fashion statement. In the 1300s, it was considered fashionable for European men to wear shoes with extremely long toes. On some of these shoes, called *crackowes*, the toe was so long that it had to be fastened to the knee with a chain so that the wearer would not trip. In the 1970s, *platform shoes*, with very thick soles, were popular. What shoe styles are popular today?

At a Glance

Grouping: Pairs or Small Groups

Launch

- Have a class discussion about what measurements a shoe company would be interested in knowing.

- Discuss how these measurements might be found.

Explore

- Have students trace their feet, make their measurements, and record their data in a class table.

Summarize

- Discuss the follow-up questions and any outliers in the class data.

- Ask questions to encourage students to focus on measurement strategies.

Assignment Choices

ACE questions 1–24 (1 requires string; 16 requires a city or state map; 17–21 require a world atlas or encyclopedia; 22 and 23 require a transparency of centimeter grid paper) and unassigned choices from earlier problems

Problem 2.1

With your group, have a discussion about measuring feet. In what ways can you measure a foot? Which of these measurements would be of interest to shoe companies?

Have each person in your group trace one foot on a piece of grid paper.

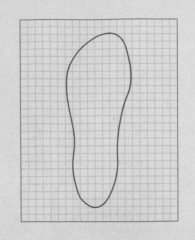

For each person's foot, estimate the length, width, area, perimeter, and any other measures your group thinks should be included. Record your data in a table with these column headings:

Student	Shoe size	Foot length	Foot width	Foot area	Foot perimeter

■ Problem 2.1 Follow-Up

Use the data from the whole class to answer these questions.

1. Does each of the data items seem reasonable? If there are outliers, do they indicate mistakes, or interesting feet?

2. **a.** What are the typical length, width, perimeter, and area of feet for students in your class?

   b. Explain how you organized the data and what measure(s) of center you used to decide what is typical.

3. Explain any patterns you see that would help you to predict shoe size from a particular foot measurement.

Answers to Problem 2.1

Answers will vary.

Answers to Problem 2.1 Follow-Up

1. The answer depends on the class data. A data point that is much larger or smaller than the other data points may signal a mistake or may be an interesting foot.

2a. The answer depends on the class data and the measurement(s) students use to describe the typical length, width, perimeter, and area of a foot.

Applications • Connections • Extensions

As you work on these ACE questions, use your calculator whenever you need it.

Applications

1. Below is a tracing of a student's hand on centimeter grid paper. The drawing has been reduced.

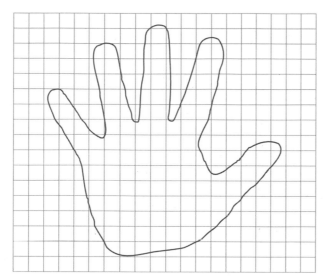

   a. Estimate the area of the student's hand.

   b. Use a piece of string or another method that makes sense to you to estimate the perimeter of the student's hand.

   c. Explain how a company that makes gloves might be interested in area and perimeter of hands.

   d. If the student's hand had been traced on half-centimeter grid paper, would your estimates be more precise, the same, or less precise? Explain.

Investigation 2: Measuring Odd Shapes 21

Answers

Applications

1a. The area is somewhere between 102 and 118 square centimeters.

1b. The perimeter is somewhere between 77 and 87 centimeters.

1c. Twice the area of a hand plus a little more for the thickness of the hand would give a manufacturer some idea of how much material is needed for one glove. The perimeter would be a good estimate for the amount of thread needed to sew the two pieces together.

1d. The estimates would be more precise. The smaller the square units, the less "putting together" of pieces is needed to make complete squares. Also, because the pieces are smaller, there is less area formed by putting together squares to make whole units and thus less chance for error.

2b. In addition to a table, students may use a line plot or coordinate graph to organize the class data. Students may describe what is typical about feet in your class by giving the median, mode, mean, or intervals where the data cluster.

3. See page 28c.

2. Ghost Lake, because it has the longer shoreline. Ghost Lake's shoreline is about 25 kilometers; Loon Lake's shoreline is about 14 kilometers.

3. Both lakes have an area of 12 to 14 square kilometers, but Loon Lake has more open area for fast boating. Ghost Lake has many twists and turns.

4. Ghost Lake could accommodate the greatest number of lakeside campsites, because it has a longer shoreline.

5. It appears that Ghost Lake has the longest stretch without a turn, so it may be better.

In 2–7, use the map below. The Parks and Recreation Department bought a piece of property with two large lakes. Park planners proposed that one lake be used for swimming, fishing, and boating. The other lake would be a nature preserve with only hiking, tent camping, and canoes allowed.

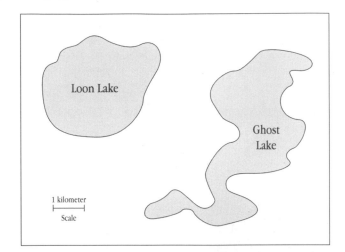

2. Naturalists claim that water birds need long shorelines for nesting and fishing. Which lake best meets this requirement? Explain your answer.

3. Boaters want a lake with a large area to give them space to cruise. Which lake best meets this requirement? Explain your answer.

4. Which lake has space for the greatest number of lakeside campsites? Explain your answer.

5. People who race powerboats like long stretches of water without turns. Which lake best meets this requirement? Explain your answer.

Tips for the Linguistically Diverse Classroom

Visual Enhancement The Visual Enhancement technique is described in detail in *Getting to Know Connected Mathematics*. It involves using real objects or pictures to make information comprehensible. Example: While discussing the questions on this page, you might show pictures of a lake with campsites, hiking trails, water birds, and power boats.

6. Sailors like lakes with long stretches to enable them to sail with any wind direction. Which lake best meets this requirement? Explain your answer.

7. Which lake do you think would be best to use for swimming, boating, and fishing, and which would be best for the nature preserve? Prepare an argument defending your choices.

Connections

8. The table below gives data on measures of head circumference (the distance around the head) and waist circumference (the distance around the waist) for 20 students.

Student	Head circumference (inches)	Waist circumference (inches)
M.S.	21.5	29.5
C.A.	23.5	32
P.B.	22	27.5
G.L.	23.25	26
K.B.	23	38.5
S.M.	21.5	23.5
K.E.	22.5	29.5
B.D.	23	27
J.G.	21	27
P.N.	21.5	28.5
L.C.	23	28
J.Y.	22	25
R.M.	21	26
J.H.	21.5	25
M.N.	23.5	25.5
M.L.	20.5	23
W.S.	20.5	31
J.J.	22	22
B.A.	23.5	31
C.F.	22.5	35

6. Loon Lake might be better for sailing because it has more room for navigating and maneuvering. With a constant wind, though, either lake would probably do well.

7. Answers will vary. Based on the answers above, Loon Lake would probably be best for swimming, boating, and fishing; Ghost Lake would probably be best for a nature preserve.

8a. See page 28c.

8b. In most cases, the head measurement is a few inches less than the waist measurement. Students may say that there is no real connection between waist circumference and head circumference. Head circumference is more or less fixed while waist circumference can vary greatly over a person's lifetime.

8c. A waist size of 30 inches is likely to be associated with a head circumference of 22 inches or more. Those who have head measures near 24 inches all have waist measures greater than 25.

8d. A waist size of 25 inches or more is likely since, once you pass 22 on the head axis, all points are higher than 25 on the waist axis.

9. The length of a belt is related to waist circumference.

10. The waist size of a pair of jeans is related to waist and hip circumference.

11. Hat size is related to head circumference.

12. Shirt size is related to neck, arm, and chest circumference.

13. You need to know the area of the walls to determine how much paint to buy.

14. You need to know the area available and the dimensions of the lot to

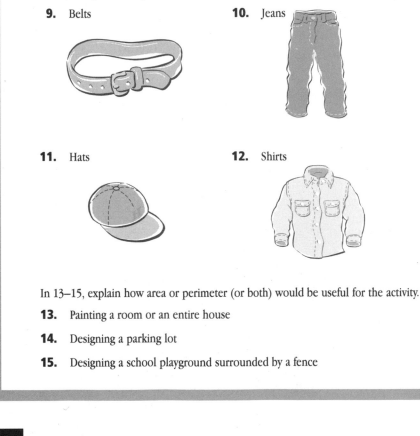

a. Make a coordinate graph with waist circumference on the horizontal axis and head circumference on the vertical axis.

b. Do you think there is a relationship between head circumference and waist circumference? Why or why not?

c. What would be a good estimate for the head circumference of a student with a waist circumference of 30 inches?

d. What would be a good estimate for the waist circumference of a student with a head circumference of 24 inches?

In 9–12, explain how perimeter is related to the size of each item.

9. Belts

10. Jeans

11. Hats

12. Shirts

In 13–15, explain how area or perimeter (or both) would be useful for the activity.

13. Painting a room or an entire house

14. Designing a parking lot

15. Designing a school playground surrounded by a fence

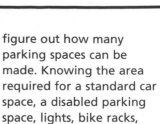

Extensions

16. Find a map of your city or state. Use the map's scale to estimate the area and the length of the border of your city or state.

In 17–21, use a world atlas or an encyclopedia to answer the question.

17. What is the world's longest river? What type of measurement was used to determine that it is the longest?

18. What is the world's largest lake? What type of measurement was used to determine that it is the largest?

19. Which country is the largest in the world? What type of measurement was used to determine that it is the largest?

20. What is the world's tallest mountain? What type of measurement was used to determine that it is the tallest?

21. What is the worlds' largest island? What type of measurement was used to determine that it is the largest?

figure out how many parking spaces can be made. Knowing the area required for a standard car space, a disabled parking space, lights, bike racks, and other parking-lot items will help you to lay out the lot.

15. You will need to know how much area (space) is available to build the playground. You need the perimeter to figure out how much fencing to buy.

16. Answers will depend on the map, the area chosen, and the scale used.

17. the Amazon (4195 miles); length

18. Lake Superior (31,800 square miles); area

19. Russia (6,592,800 square miles); area

20. Mt. Everest (29,029 feet); length (height)

21. Australia (2,914,526 square miles); area

22. Possible answer: The perimeter of Lake Okeehele is about 2800 feet, so there can be approximately 28 building sites.

23. By using a centimeter grid, you can estimate that the current area of the lake is approximately 410,000 square feet, which is less than the 500,000 square feet in 1920. It seems the lake is shrinking.

24. The measurements were probably determined partly by measuring and partly by estimating. (This kind of estimation is often done from aerial photographs in which the scale of the photograph can be determined.)

In 22 and 23, use this map of Lake Okeehele and a centimeter grid transparency.

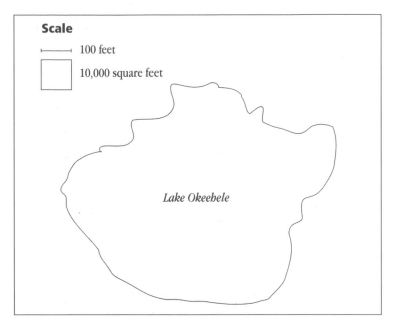

22. A developer plans to build houses around Lake Okeehele. If most of his customers want to buy about 100 feet of lakefront, how many lots can the developer build around the lake? Explain your answer.

23. The buyers want to know whether the lake has shrunk or grown over time. The developer found in the county records that the lake covered 500,000 square feet in 1920. What is happening to the lake? Give evidence to support your answer.

24. The state of Hawaii is a group of islands. Atlases and almanacs report the area of Hawaii as 6450 square miles and the shoreline as 1052 miles. How do you think these measurements were made? You might want to ask your geography teacher for more information.

Did you know?

The islands of Hawaii were formed from the eruptions of many volcanoes over tens of thousands of years. Volcanoes in the island chain are still erupting today—both above and below the water. Volcanoes continually add new land to Hawaii, so the area and perimeter of the state are increasing. Someday the buildup of hardened volcanic matter under the ocean will emerge as a new Hawaiian island.

Possible Answers

1. If the shape is on grid paper, you can find the area by counting whole squares and fractional parts of squares. If the shape isn't on a grid, you can put a transparent grid over the shape and count squares. To find perimeter, you can figure out what length of string is needed to enclose the outside of the object, then measure the string with a ruler.

2. Not necessarily. Although students did not directly investigate this idea, they should be able to transfer what they learned in Investigation 1 to nongeometric shapes.

3. No. Students should be able to talk about the fact that area can be put together lots of ways and the way the area is arranged affects the shape's perimeter.

Mathematical Reflections

In this investigation, you examined areas and perimeters of odd shapes using square grids and grid paper. These questions will help you summarize what you have learned:

1 Describe how you can find the area and perimeter of an odd shape such as a footprint.

2 If two odd shapes have the same perimeter, do they have the same area?

3 Can you figure out the perimeter of an odd shape if you know its area? Why or why not?

Think about your answers to these questions, discuss your ideas with other students and your teacher, and then write a summary of your findings in your journal.

What objects in a park might have odd shapes—a flower garden? A picnic area? A play area?

Tips for the Linguistically Diverse Classroom

Original Rebus The Original Rebus technique is described in detail in *Getting to Know Connected Mathematics*. Students make a copy of the text before it is discussed. During discussion, they generate their own rebuses for words they do not understand as the words are made comprehensible through pictures, objects, or demonstrations. Example: Question 1—key words for which students may make rebuses are *area* (a shape with the area inside shaded), *perimeter* (the bold outline of a shape), *footprint* (a footprint).

TEACHING THE INVESTIGATION

2.1 • Making the Shoe Fit

In this problem, students estimate the perimeter and area of irregular shapes: tracings of their feet.

Launch

Ask students what measurements of feet they think a shoe company would need to know. Record the measurements students suggest on the board, along with an explanation of why each might be important to a shoe company. If students do not include the measurements that are suggested in the problem (shoe size, foot length, foot width, foot perimeter, and foot area), suggest that they be included.

Ask students to explain how they might find these measurements. Since length and width are part of the data students are collecting, someone may suggest that you multiply them to get area of a foot. If so, ask students for what shape is multiplying the length and width an appropriate way to find area. Then ask if their foot is a rectangle. You may want to suggest that they test this method by *counting* the number of square units that make up the area of the bottom of their foot and comparing the answer to that arrived at by multiplication.

Each student will trace one foot on centimeter grid paper. (For hygiene reasons, have them keep their socks on. If you think having students remove their shoes in class will be a problem, you could ask them to do the tracing at home the evening before.) Explain that they will use their tracings to make their measurements and to refer to when explaining how they determined each measurement.

Explore

This problem can be done in pairs or groups of three. Have string and rulers available for students to use for measuring. Make a table on the board or overhead projector for recording foot measurements.

As you circulate, make sure students are thinking about what they are measuring and how they are determining their measurements. After making the measurements, students can compare measurements within their group and discuss whether they are reasonable. When the group agrees their measurements are reasonable, have them record their numbers in the class table.

Summarize

Start the summary by talking about the follow-up questions. If there are outliers that appear to be measuring errors, ask the student who recorded the value how he or she made the measurement. Have the class discuss whether the method is reasonable.

Pose additional questions to focus the discussion on measurement strategies.

> Explain the strategies you used to find the length of your foot. Did anyone do it another way? What did you do if your length measured part of a unit? (*Students should be able to use their knowledge of fractions from the last unit to determine a reasonable measurement, including fractions of a unit.*)

Explain the strategies you used to find the width of your foot. Did anyone do it another way? What did you do if your width measured part of a unit?

Explain the strategies you used to find area. Did anyone do it another way? What did you do with parts of squares?

Explain the strategies you used to find perimeter. Did anyone do it another way?

If we had used a smaller grid to measure our feet, the numbers would have changed, but would your estimates be more precise, the same, or less precise? Explain your thinking.

For the Teacher: Using Smaller Grids

If students had used half-centimeter grid paper, it would take four of the smaller squares to equal one of the larger squares.

While this mathematics is probably too sophisticated for most grade 6 students, the idea that small units give a better estimate than larger units can be seen by looking at how much of the foot is covered by whole units in each case. You can see that on the half-centimeter grid, more of the foot is covered with whole squares, leaving less room for error.

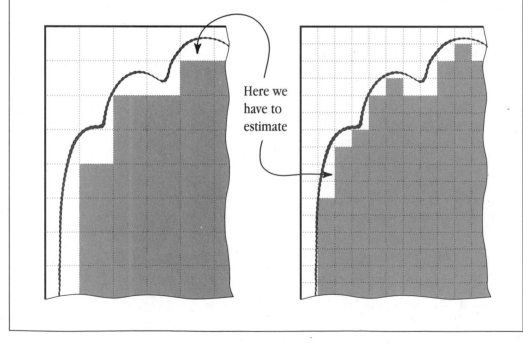

Here we have to estimate

Additional Answers

Answers to Problem 2.1 Follow-Up

3. Students may find a relationship between foot length and shoe size. Some classes also study shoe width (AA, A, B, C, etc.) and look for a relationship between the width of students' feet and the width of their shoes.

ACE Answers

Applications

8a.

Head and Waist Measurements

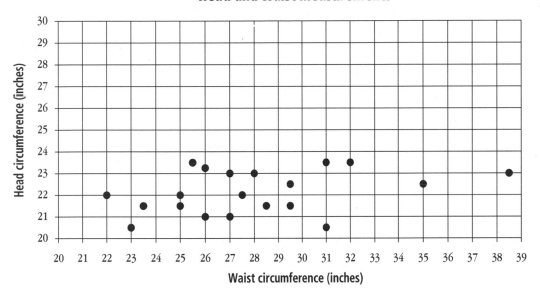

Constant Area, Changing Perimeter

In this investigation, students develop the formula for the area of a rectangle. Few students see the pattern or can articulate the formula for the perimeter of a rectangle. This will be developed in Investigation 4. This investigation also sets the stage for finding areas of parallelograms (in Investigation 5) and triangles (in Investigation 6).

Problem 3.1, Building Storm Shelters, asks students to find all the possible rectangular floor plans for shelters with an area of 24 square meters. They make their designs with tiles, organize their information in a table, and look for patterns. In most classrooms, the formula for the area of a rectangle and an understanding of why the formula works result from the summary discussion for this problem. In Problem 3.2, Stretching the Perimeter, students continue to investigate perimeters for a constant area of 24 square units, but they are no longer restricted to rectangular arrangements.

Holding one variable (in this case, area) constant to study how another variable (in this case, perimeter) changes is a powerful mathematical tool used to analyze a wide variety of problems.

Mathematical and Problem-Solving Goals

■ *To understand how the perimeters of rectangles can vary considerably even when the area is held constant*

■ *To construct diagrams and tables to organize and represent data*

■ *To explore maxima/minima questions in the context of finding the largest and smallest perimeters for rectangles of a fixed area*

■ *To continue to develop a conceptual understanding of area and perimeter*

Materials		
Problem	**For students**	**For the teacher**
All	Calculators, centimeter grid paper (provided as a blackline master)	Transparencies 3.1 and 3.2 (optional)
3.1	Square tiles (24 per student)	
3.2	String, scissors	4×6 rectangle cut from inch grid paper

Student Pages　　　Teaching the Investigation

INVESTIGATION **3**

Constant Area, Changing Perimeter

In making floor plans for anything from a doghouse to a dream house, you have many options. Even when area and perimeter are fixed, there are lots of possible floor plans. Many factors—including the cost of materials and the purposes of the rooms—help to determine the best possible plan.

3.1 Building Storm Shelters

From March 12–14, 1993, a fierce winter storm hit the eastern United States from Florida to Maine. Thousands of people were stranded in the snow, far from shelter. A group of 24 Michigan students, who had been hiking in the Smoky Mountains of Tennessee, were among those stranded.

To prepare for this kind of emergency, parks often provide shelters at points along major hiking trails. Since the shelters are only for emergency use, they are designed to be simple and inexpensive buildings that are easily maintained.

Investigation 3: Constant Area, Changing Perimeter **29**

Tips for the Linguistically Diverse Classroom

Visual Enhancement The Visual Enhancement technique is described in detail in *Getting to Know Connected Mathematics*. It involves using real objects or pictures to make information comprehensible. Example: While discussing the material on this page, you might show pictures of a blizzard, a mountain range, and a simple storm shelter.

3.1

Building Storm Shelters

Launch

- Help students understand the mathematical context of the problem.

Explore

- Have students work on the problem, individually or in pairs.

Summarize

- As a class, record students' findings.

- Talk about any patterns students notice.

- If students discover the formula for the area of a rectangle, have them verify that it works for rectangles of other dimensions.

Assignment Choices

ACE questions 1–6 and unassigned choices from earlier problems

Stretching the Perimeter

At a Glance

***Grouping:
Individuals, then
Small Groups***

Launch

- Demonstrate how to make a nonrectangular shape with an area of 24 square units.

Explore

- Have students make their own nonrectangular shapes and determine their perimeters.

- Ask students who finish early to try making a shape with a greater perimeter.

- Display the students' shapes along with the strings cut to show the perimeter of each shape. (*optional*)

Summarize

- As a class, discuss the shapes and their perimeters.

- Have students share strategies for creating a shape with a larger perimeter.

Problem 3.1

The rangers in Great Smoky Mountains National Park want to build several inexpensive storm shelters. The shelters must have 24 square meters of floor space. Suppose that the walls are made of sections that are 1 meter wide and cost $125.

A. Use your tiles to experiment with different rectangular shapes. Sketch each possible floor plan on grid paper. Record your group's data in a table with these column headings:

    Length   Width   Perimeter   Area   Cost of walls

B. Based on the cost of the wall sections, which design would be the least expensive to build? Describe what that shelter would look like.

C. Which shelter plan has the most expensive set of wall sections? Describe what that shelter would look like.

■ Problem 3.1 Follow-Up

Can you find a design—other than a rectangle—with 24 square meters of floor space and lower wall-section costs than any of the designs you have looked at so far? Experiment with your tiles to answer this question.

3.2 Stretching the Perimeter

In Problem 3.1, you worked with rectangles to help you understand the relationship between area and perimeter. In this problem, you will look at what happens when you cut an interesting part from a rectangle and slide that piece onto another edge. Look at these examples:

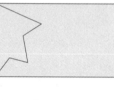
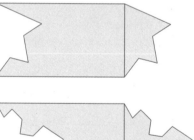

Assignment Choices

ACE questions 7 and 8 and unassigned choices from earlier problems

Answers to Problem 3.1

A. See the table on page 34b.

B. The 4 × 6 (or 6 × 4) shelter is the least expensive to build. This floor plan is the most square-like of the possibilities. The shelter would have the most open space and the fewest wall sections.

C. The 1 × 24 (or 24 × 1) shelter is the most expensive to build. The floor plan is long and skinny, with the least open space and the most wall sections.

Answer to Problem 3.1 Follow-Up

See page 34e.

Can you use this techique to find a nonrectangular shape with an area of 24 square units and a larger perimeter than any of the rectangles you've found?

Problem 3.2

Draw a 4×6 rectangle on grid paper, and cut it out.

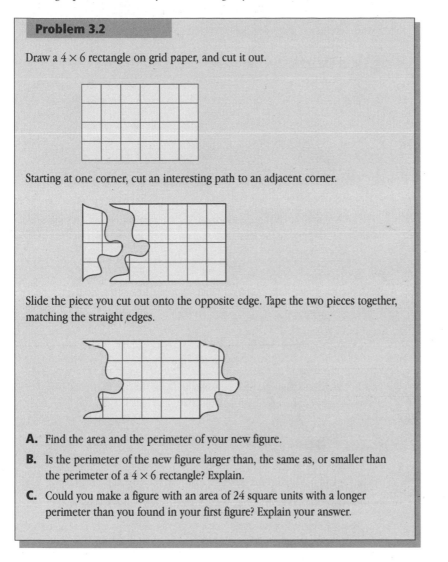

Starting at one corner, cut an interesting path to an adjacent corner.

Slide the piece you cut out onto the opposite edge. Tape the two pieces together, matching the straight edges.

A. Find the area and the perimeter of your new figure.

B. Is the perimeter of the new figure larger than, the same as, or smaller than the perimeter of a 4×6 rectangle? Explain.

C. Could you make a figure with an area of 24 square units with a longer perimeter than you found in your first figure? Explain your answer.

■ **Problem 3.2 Follow-Up**

Summarize what you have discovered about figures with an area of 24 square units.

Answers to Problem 3.2

A. Areas will all be 24 square units; perimeters will be 20 units or greater.

B. Possible answer: The perimeter of the rectangle is 20 units. The perimeters of the new figures are all greater than 20 units, because when you cut and move the piece, more edge is exposed.

C. Possible answer: Yes, by removing a piece from the rectangle with a longer cut edge.

Answer to Problem 3.2 Follow-Up

Possible answer: Figures with an area of 24 square meters come in lots of shapes. If you consider only rectangles with whole-number side lengths, there are four possible shapes. If you allow any shape, there are many possibilities. The perimeter will depend on how stretched-out the shape is and how much edge is exposed.

ACE

Answers

Applications

1. See page 34f.

2. The design with the smallest perimeter, and thus costing the least, would be a 4 × 5 rectangle. It is the most square-like of the possible designs. If we allow edges that are not whole numbers, the best design is a square of about 4.47 (the square root of 20) units on an edge.

3. A 6 × 6 square, which has a perimeter of 24 square units.

4. A square 4 feet on a side would require the least amount of material (the perimeter would be 16 feet).

5. The rectangle with the greatest perimeter is a 1 × 36 rectangle, with a perimeter—or seating capacity—of 74 units.

6a. 1 × 60, 2 × 30, 3 × 20, 4 × 15, 5 × 12, and 6 × 10

6b. 1 × 61

6c. 1 × 62 and 2 × 31

6d. The factors of a number and the dimensions of the rectangles that can be made from that number of tiles are the same. For example, the factors of 62 are 1, 2, 31, and 62.

As you work on these ACE questions, use your calculator whenever you need it.

Applications

1. Sketch all the rectangles with an area of 30 square units and whole-number side lengths.

2. If the park rangers in Problem 3.1 wanted to build storm shelters with 20 square meters of floor space instead of 24, what design would be the least expensive?

3. Find the rectangle with an area 36 square units and whole-number side lengths that has the smallest perimeter possible.

4. Alyssa is designing a rectangular sandbox. The bottom is to cover 16 square feet. What shape will require the least amount of material for the sides of the sandbox?

5. Suppose you wanted to make a large banquet table from 36 square card tables. Four people can be seated at a card table, one person on each side. With two card tables put together to make a larger table, six people can be seated:

How would you arrange the 36 card tables to make the banquet table seat the greatest number of people? Explain your reasoning.

Connections

6. In a–c, find all rectangles that can be made from the given number of tiles.

   a. 60 square tiles   **b.** 61 square tiles   **c.** 62 square tiles

   d. How can you use your work in a–c to list the factors of 60, 61, and 62?

Extensions

7. A *pentomino* is a shape made of five identical squares that are connected along straight edges.

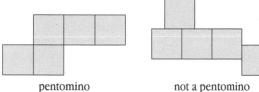

pentomino   not a pentomino

Turning or flipping a pentomino does *not* make a different pentomino.

a. Find all the possible pentominos. On grid paper, sketch each pentomino that you find.

b. Why do you think you have found all the possible pentominos?

c. Which pentomino has the smallest perimeter? Which pentomino has the largest perimeter?

8. a. On grid paper, design a 120-square-foot bedroom that you would enjoy having for your own. Draw in furniture on your floor plan. Measure real rooms, closets, and furniture to see whether your design is reasonable. Record the measurements you find. Include measures for a bed and a dresser.

b. Describe why you think your design would be a good design for a bedroom. Include how you decided what would be reasonable for the shape of the room, the size of closets, and the other features of your design.

Extensions

7a. See page 34f.

7b. Possible answer: I conducted a systematic search.

7c. This pentomino has the smallest perimeter, 10 units, because four of the tiles have two edges joined. All of the other pentominos have a perimeter of 12 units.

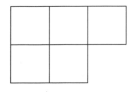

8a. Answers will vary. This problem gives students a chance to use ideas about area and perimeter in a real-life situation.

8b. Answers will vary.

Possible Answers

1. By now all students should answer no to this question and be able to refer to the rectangles and other figures they constructed with an area of 24 square units but varying perimeters. For example, a 4×6 rectangle has a perimeter of 20 units, and a 2×12 rectangle has a perimeter of 28 units; both have an area of 24 square units.

2. The most square-like rectangle will have the smallest perimeter. It will be the most compact and have the fewest number of exposed edges.

3. The "skinniest" rectangle will have the largest perimeter. The tiles for the skinny rectangle will only touch on one or two edges, so lots of edges will be exposed.

Mathematical Reflections

In this investigation, you designed storm shelters with an area of 24 square meters and determined which design would cost the least because it had the smallest perimeter. This problem helped you see how the perimeters of rectangles made from the same number of tiles can vary. You also looked at the perimeters of nonrectangular shapes with an area of 24 square units. These questions will help you summarize what you have learned:

1 If two rectangles have the same area, must they also have the same perimeter? Explain your answer.

2 Of all possible rectangles with a given area and whole-number side lengths, which has the smallest perimeter?

3 Of all possible rectangles with a given area and whole-number side lengths, which has the largest perimeter?

Think about your answers to these questions, discuss your ideas with other students and your teacher, and then write a summary of your findings in your journal.

Think about the city park you will be designing. You will have to use part of the area of the park for picnic tables, playground equipment, and other attractions. How could what you have learned about the relationship of perimeter and area be useful to you? You might want to visit some local parks to get more ideas for how you will design your city park. You may also want to measure some things in the parks you visit so you have a good idea about what size things in your design should be. Don't forget to record everything you find out!

34 Covering and Surrounding

Tips for the Linguistically Diverse Classroom

Diagram Code The Diagram Code technique is described in detail in *Getting to Know Connected Mathematics*. Students use a minimal number of words and drawings, diagrams, or symbols to respond to questions that require writing. Example: Question 3—A student might answer this question by drawing a long skinny rectangle made from tiles with arrows pointing to where the first few tiles touch and the words only *touch 1 or 2 sides*.

TEACHING THE INVESTIGATION

3.1 • Building Storm Shelters

In this problem, students find all the possible rectangles with whole number side lengths and a perimeter of 24 square units.

Launch

Before they begin working on the problem, help students understand the mathematical context.

> We have been finding areas and perimeters of several shapes. In this problem we will look at a specific shape, a rectangle. We want to find all the rectangles that can be made with a given area.

Ask students to use 12 of their tiles to build a rectangle.

> Tell me what you built by giving me the length and width of your rectangle, which are called the *dimensions* of the rectangle. Also give the perimeter and area of your rectangle.

Record the length, width, perimeter, and area of each rectangle on the board. Continue collecting examples until all possibilities have been found. If you include reversals—such as 1×12 and 12×1—there are six possibilities. Many students do consider a 1×12 rectangle and a 12×1 rectangle to be different. If this is true in your class, we suggest that you collect both possibilities and then ask questions that encourage students to recognize that the perimeters and areas are the same and to think about why this is so. You want students to understand that these are the same rectangle with different orientations. If students are giving answers with reversals, they may still be confused about this idea. Take this opportunity to discuss it again.

Length	Width	Area	Perimeter
1 unit	12 units	12 square units	26 units
2 units	6 units	12 square units	16 units
3 units	4 units	12 square units	14 units
4 units	3 units	12 square units	14 units
6 units	2 units	12 square units	16 units
12 units	1 unit	12 square units	26 units

> How do you know we have found all the rectangles that can be made using 12 tiles?

Students may say that all the possible factor pairs have been given as lengths and widths.

Read the story about the winter storm and the problem of building storm shelters with your class. Make sure students understand the problem.

> As you work on this problem, record your findings in a table similar to the one we used to find all the rectangles with an area of 12 square units. You will need to add a column for cost.

Explore

The launch and the work students did on a similar problem in the *Prime Time* unit have pre-pared them to work alone or in pairs to sketch and record their findings on this problem.

Make sure students are making sketches as well as completing the chart. Some students may choose not to use tiles because they can see patterns without them. This is fine. Using tiles to make models of the shelters should not be a mandate; tiles are simply a tool to help make sense of the problem.

Summarize

You might begin the summary by collecting the data students recorded.

> Did anyone find a shelter design with a side length of 1 meter? What is the width of that shelter? What is the perimeter? You know it has an area of 24 square meters, because that was required. What is the cost of the walls for this shelter design?

> Did anyone find a shelter design with a side length of 2 meters? What is the width of that shelter? What is the perimeter? What is the cost of the walls for that shelter?

Continue with this line of questions for side lengths of 3, 4, 5, 6, 7, 8, 12, and 24. Asking for side lengths of 5 and 7 should give rise to a short discussion about factors. If students state that they don't need to list 6, 8, 12, and 24 because they are reversals, then stop listing, but be sure to ask them how they know they have found all possible rectangles.

> Look at the table we have generated. What patterns do you notice? Explain why each pattern you see makes sense.

Length	Width	Perimeter	Area	Cost of Walls
1 meter	24 meters	50 meters	24 square meters	$6250
2 meters	12 meters	28 meters	24 square meters	$3500
3 meters	8 meters	22 meters	24 square meters	$2750
4 meters	6 meters	20 meters	24 square meters	$2500
6 meters	4 meters	20 meters	24 square meters	$2500
8 meters	3 meters	22 meters	24 square meters	$2750
12 meters	2 meters	28 meters	24 square meters	$3500
24 meters	1 meter	50 meters	24 square meters	$6250

Here are some patterns students have noticed.

- Fiona said that the area is always 24 square meters.

- Nathan said that as one dimension gets larger, the other gets smaller. (If you put more square tiles in a row, you must have fewer rows, since in all cases you have 24 tiles.)

- Erik noticed that opposites have the same measures—a 3 × 8 rectangle and an 8 × 3 rectangle have the same perimeter and cost. (They are really the same rectangle; one is a 90° rotation of the other.)

■ Mari discovered that the length and width multiplied together give you 24, which is the area. (Since the length tells you how many tiles are in a row and the width tells you how many rows, multiplying the length by the width gives the number of tiles, or square units, in the rectangle.)

If students discover the formula for finding the area of a rectangle, ask them to work with another student (so that 48 tiles will be available) to try their rule on a few other rectangles—for example, a rectangle with a length of 7 units and a width of 3 units; a length of 5 units and a width of 8 units; a length of 6 units and a width of 8 units. Ask students to build these rectangles and check that the pattern for finding area works for all of them.

For the Teacher: Developing A Perimeter Formula

At this point, it is unlikely that a pattern for perimeter will emerge; don't press for it if it doesn't. In Problem 4.1, students will investigate holding perimeter constant and finding all possible areas. This activity will help them uncover the pattern and develop the formula for the perimeter of a rectangle on their own.

Encourage students to visualize what the shelters with the largest and smallest perimeters look like.

Which of the shelters with an area of 24 square meters has the largest perimeter? (*1 × 24*) What does this shelter look like? (*It is long and skinny.*) How much do the walls for this design cost? (*$6250*) Would this make a good shelter? (*No. It would be uncomfortable for people to stay in, because it is not very wide. Also, the walls cost more than the walls for the other shelters, so it is not an inexpensive design.*)

Which of the shelters with an area of 24 square meters has the smallest perimeter? (*4 × 6*) What does it look like? (*It's more square-like.*) How much do the walls for this design cost? (*$2500*) Would this make a good shelter? Explain your reasoning. (*Yes. It would give a lot of open space, and its walls cost the least.*)

For the Teacher: Using Fractional Side Lengths

If we allow sides that are not whole numbers, the best design is a square with side lengths of about 4.9 (the square root of 24) units.

If you were going to construct a rectangular shelter with an area of 36 square units, which design would cost the most to build? Why?

Help students to see that a 1 × 36 shelter would cost the most. This shelter has the greatest perimeter of any other arrangement of 36 square tiles, so it would require the most wall sections and have the highest cost.

If you were going to build a rectangular shelter with an area of
36 square units, which design would cost the least to build? Why?

The 6 × 6 shelter would be the least expensive, because it is the most compact and therefore has
the smallest perimeter (24 units). In the tile models, this arrangement of tiles has the fewest
exposed edges to contribute to the perimeter.

You may choose to make the follow-up a homework assignment so students have time to investigate possibilities.

3.2 • Stretching the Perimeter

In this problem, students continue to investigate perimeters for a constant area of 24 square
units; however, they are no longer restricted to rectangles. The question in this problem is:
Can you make a shape with a larger perimeter than a rectangle with the same area?

Launch

Read the problem with the class. Model the procedure with a 4 × 6 rectangle, cutting it as
described in the student edition. Slide your piece and tape it to the opposite edge.

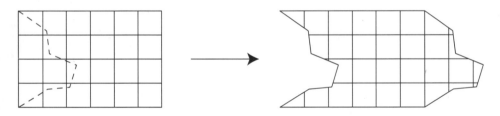

What is the area of this new shape? How do you know? (*The area is still
24 square units, the area of the original rectangle.*) How can we find
the perimeter of this shape? (*The lengths of the straight edges are 6
units each. You can use string to find the lengths of the other edges.*)
How do area and perimeter of this new shape compare with the area
and perimeter of the 4 × 6 rectangle? (*The area is the same but the
perimeter is larger.*)

Once students understand the issue, let them work on the problem.

Explore

Students should make their own shapes and answer the questions individually, then meet with
their groups to share and compare answers. As students work, make sure they are taking time to
measure accurately enough to see the differences in perimeters. Suggest that students who finish
early try to make another figure with an even greater perimeter than the one they just made. Ask
what strategy they are using to accomplish this task.

You could have students cut string the length of the perimeter of their figures. Later, you could display the shapes and their perimeters—the lengths of string—to help students better visualize the relationship between constant area and changing perimeter.

Summarize

Have groups share their findings. Focus on the fact that every new figure has an area of 24 square units, yet the perimeters vary.

Have students share the strategies they discovered for making figures with greater perimeters.

Additional Answers

Answer to Problem 3.1 Follow-Up

The 4 × 6 shelter is the least expensive design that can be built using whole-number meters for the lengths of sides. You can build shapes with the same perimeter as the 4 × 6 rectangle, but none with a smaller perimeter. For example:

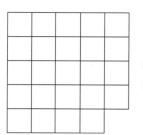

area = 24 square units
perimeter = 20 units

ACE Answers

Applications

1.

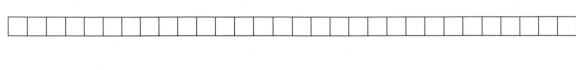

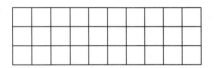

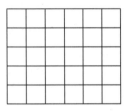

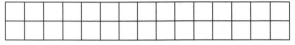

Extensions

7a. There are 12 pentominos.

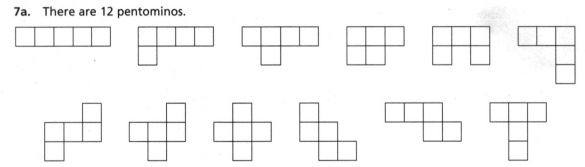

Constant Perimeter, Changing Area

In Investigation 3, students began with a fixed area and investigated how the perimeter could vary. In this investigation, students begin with a fixed perimeter and explore how the area can vary. It is important that students get a sense of which variable is held fixed and which is allowed to change. As with the last investigation, this investigation begins with an open-ended problem.

Problem 4.1, Fencing in Spaces, asks students to find all the ways to make a dog pen with whole-number side lengths from 24 meters of fencing. Students use tiles to model the pens and record the results in a table. While looking for patterns in their tables, they discover the maximum and minimum possible areas for a rectangle with a perimeter of 24 units. In Problem 4.2, Adding Tiles to Pentominos, students add tiles to a given pentomino to form shapes with a perimeter of 18 units. They discover that they can change the perimeter by 0, 2, or –2 units by adding a single tile, depending on where they add the tile.

Mathematical and Problem-Solving Goals

- *To learn that the areas of rectangles with a fixed perimeter can vary considerably*

- *To construct diagrams and tables to organize and represent data*

- *To find the minimum and maximum areas of rectangles with a fixed perimeter*

- *To distinguish the case of fixed area from the case of fixed perimeter*

- *To continue to develop a conceptual understanding of area and perimeter*

Materials		
Problem	**For students**	**For the teacher**
All	Calculators, square tiles (24 per group), centimeter grid paper (provided as a blackline master)	Transparencies 4.1 and 4.2 (optional)
ACE	Labsheet 4.ACE (for ACE question 4, 1 per student)	

Constant Perimeter, Changing Area

You often encounter situations in which you want to make the most of something. For example, suppose you were planning a party and had a set amount of money to spend on decorations and refreshments. Or, imagine that you were going on a trip and had a certain amount of spending money. In either situation, you would want to make the most of your budget.

Sometimes you want to make the least of something. If you were building a toy airplane or a racing bicycle, you would want to make it as lightweight as possible.

Mathematicians call these kinds of tasks finding the *maximum* or finding the *minimum*. In the last investigation, you found the maximum and minimum *perimeter* you could have for a rectangle with a fixed area of 24 square meters and whole-number side lengths. In this investigation, you will start with a fixed *perimeter* and try to find the maximum and minimum *area* that perimeter can enclose.

4.1 **Fencing in Spaces**

Americans have over 50 million dogs as pets. In many parts of the country—particularly in cities—there are laws against letting dogs run free. Many people build pens so their dogs have a chance to get outside for fresh air and exercise.

Investigation 4: Constant Perimeter, Changing Area **35**

4.1

Fencing in Spaces

- - - - - - - - - - - -
At a Glance

Grouping:
Individuals or Pairs

Launch

■ Demonstrate how to find rectangles with a fixed perimeter such as 12.

Explore

■ Have students work on the problem, individually or in pairs.

■ If any students seem frustrated, make suggestions about how they might approach the problem.

Summarize

■ As a class, record students' findings and talk about any patterns they notice.

■ Discuss students' ideas on shortcuts for finding the perimeter of a rectangle.

■ Talk about the rectangles found with the smallest and largest areas.

Assignment Choices

ACE questions 1–14 (4 requires Labsheet 4.ACE; 11 requires grid paper; 14 requires inch grid paper) and unassigned choices from earlier problems

Adding Tiles to Pentominos

Launch

■ As a class, analyze the pentomino that students will be investigating.

Explore

■ If students have trouble with the follow-up, help them to develop a strategy for investigating the question.

Summarize

■ Have students share arrangements for creating a shape with the smallest and largest possible area.

■ As a class, discuss the three ways that adding a tile to the figure can affect the perimeter.

Problem 4.1

Suppose you wanted to help a friend build a rectangular pen for her dog, Shane. You have 24 meters of fencing, in 1-meter lengths, to build the pen. Which rectangular shape would be best for Shane?

Experiment with your square tiles to find all possible rectangles with a *perimeter* of 24 meters. Sketch each rectangle on grid paper. Record your data about each possible plan in a table with these column headings:

Length   Width   Perimeter   Area

■ **Problem 4.1 Follow-Up**
1. Which design would give Shane the best pen for running?
2. Which design would give Shane the most space for playing?

4.2 Adding Tiles to Pentominos

In Problem 4.1, you explored the relationship between area and perimeter by investigating the rectangles that could be made with a fixed perimeter of 24 units. In this problem, you will continue to investigate fixed perimeter by adding tiles to a pentomino.

Remember that a *pentomino* is a shape made from five identical square tiles connected along their edges. Here are some examples:

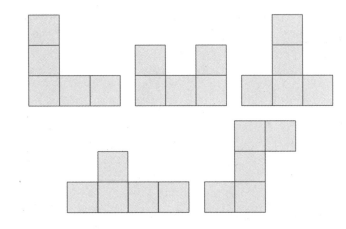

Assignment Choices

ACE question 15 and unassigned choices from earlier problems

Assessment

It is appropriate to use Check-Up 1 and Quiz A after this problem.

Answers to Problem 4.1

See the table on page 45b.

Answers to Problem 4.1 Follow-Up

1. Most students will say that the 1 × 11 pen will give Shane the longest running space, but some students may feel this narrow pen wouldn't give Shane enough space for turning around and prefer the 2 × 10 pen.

2. The 6 × 6 pen has the largest area and will give Shane the most playing space.

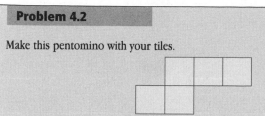

Problem 4.2

Make this pentomino with your tiles.

A. Add tiles to the pentomino to make a new figure with a perimeter of 18 units. Draw your new figure on grid paper. Show clearly where you added tiles to the pentomino.

B. What is the smallest number of tiles you can add to the pentomino to make a new figure with a perimeter of 18 units? Draw the new figure, showing where you would add tiles to the pentomino.

C. What is the largest number of tiles you can add to the pentomino to make a new figure with a perimeter of 18 units? Draw the new figure, showing where you would add tiles to the pentomino.

■ Problem 4.2 Follow-Up

How does adding one tile change the perimeter of a figure? Explain your answer. You might find it helpful to draw pictures.

Investigation 4: Constant Perimeter, Changing Area   **37**

Answers to Problem 4.2

See page 45f.

Answers to Problem 4.2 Follow-Up

Possible answer: Depending on where you add the new tile, the perimeter can increase by 2 units, stay the same, or decrease by 2 units. (See the "Summarize" section on page 45d for a more detailed explanation.)

ACE

Answers

Applications

1.

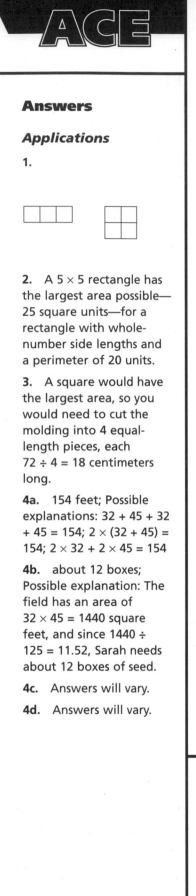

2. A 5 × 5 rectangle has the largest area possible—25 square units—for a rectangle with whole-number side lengths and a perimeter of 20 units.

3. A square would have the largest area, so you would need to cut the molding into 4 equal-length pieces, each 72 ÷ 4 = 18 centimeters long.

4a. 154 feet; Possible explanations: 32 + 45 + 32 + 45 = 154; 2 × (32 + 45) = 154; 2 × 32 + 2 × 45 = 154

4b. about 12 boxes; Possible explanation: The field has an area of 32 × 45 = 1440 square feet, and since 1440 ÷ 125 = 11.52, Sarah needs about 12 boxes of seed.

4c. Answers will vary.

4d. Answers will vary.

As you work on these ACE questions, use your calculator whenever you need it.

Applications

1. Suneeta used square tiles to make rectangles with a perimeter of 8 units. On grid paper, draw all the possible rectangles Suneeta might have made.

2. Find a rectangle with whole-number side lengths, a perimeter of 20 units, and the largest possible area.

3. If you have 72 centimeters of molding to make a frame for a painting, how should you cut the molding to give the largest possible area for the painting?

4. On the next page is a diagram of the field next to Sarah's house. Each small square represents a space that is 1 foot on each side. Sarah wants to make a garden and a play area in the field.

a. How much fencing does Sarah need to surround the field? Explain your answer.

b. A box of grass seed plants an area of 125 square feet. How many boxes of seed would Sarah need to seed the entire field? Explain your answer.

c. Sarah decides she wants to include some flower and vegetable plots and a small play area (a swing set and a sandbox) in the field. On Labsheet 4.ACE, make a design for Sarah that includes these items. Give the area and the dimensions of each part of your design.

d. How many boxes of grass seed would Sarah need to seed the design you drew for part c?

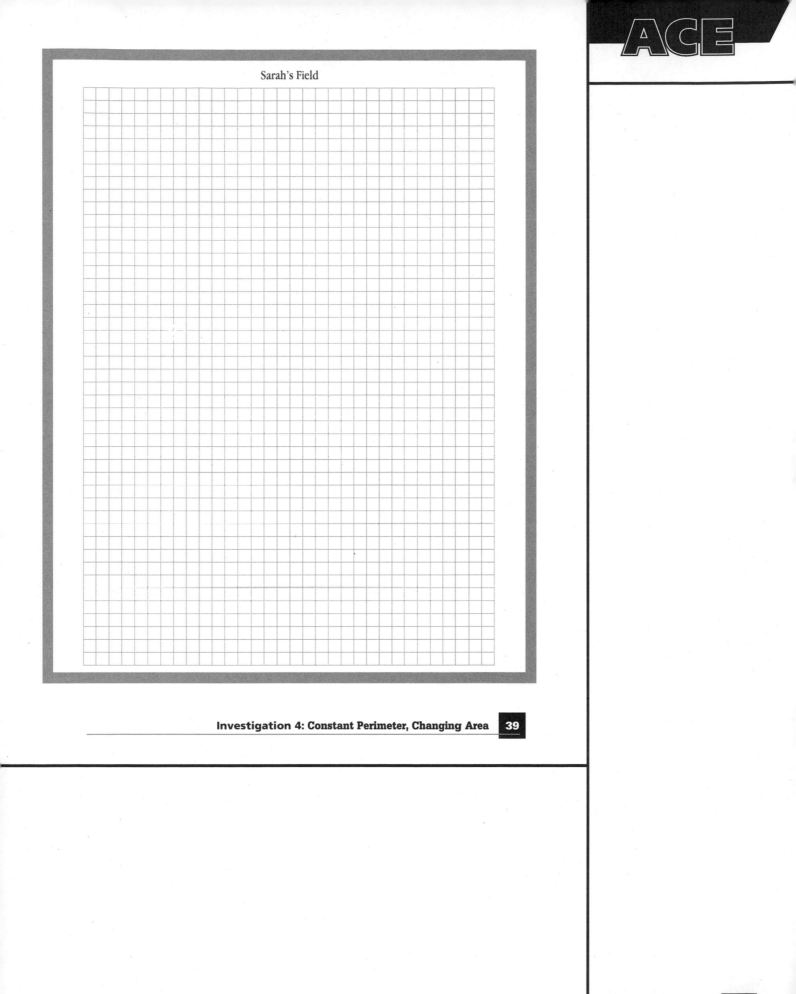

Sarah's Field

Connections

5. area = 12 square centimeters, perimeter = 16 centimeters

6. area = 10.24 square centimeters, perimeter = 12.8 centimeters

7. area = 16 square centimeters, perimeter = 16 centimeters

8. area = 8 square centimeters, perimeter = 11.4 centimeters

9a. Possible answer: The perimeters of the rectangle and the parallelogram are the same because the lengths of the sides did not change.

9b. Possible answer: The rectangle would have a larger area, because as you press the sides to make a parallelogram, it makes the shape skinnier and the area smaller. If you keep making the parallelogram skinnier, until it collapses, the area will be zero.

Connections

In 5–8, make any measurements you need to find the perimeter and area of the polygon in centimeters.

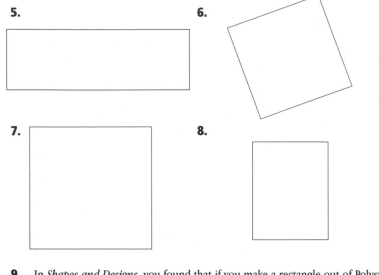

5.

6.

7.

8.

9. In *Shapes and Designs*, you found that if you make a rectangle out of Polystrips and press on the corners, the rectangle tilts out of a shape into a different parallelogram.

a. How does the perimeter of the original rectangle compare to the perimeter of the new parallelogram?

b. How does the area of the original rectangle compare to the area of the new parallelogram?

10. Kate and Eli want to design a garage with an area of 240 square feet.

a. Make an organized list showing the dimensions (length and width), in feet, of all the possible rectangular garages they could make with whole-number dimensions.

b. Which rectangles would be reasonable for a garage? Explain your answer.

c. Which rectangle would you choose for a garage? Why?

11. a. Find the perimeter and area of the rectangle below.

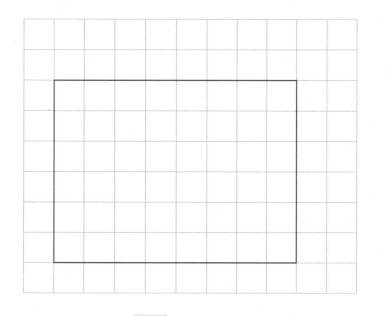

☐ = 1 square meter

10a.

Length (feet)	Width (feet)
1	240
2	120
3	80
4	60
5	48
6	40
8	30
10	24
12	20
15	16

10b. Possible answer: A car needs at least 8 feet. for the width, so the 8 × 30 design would probably be too snug. The 10 × 24, 12 × 20, and 15 × 16 designs would all be appropriate as garages.

10c. Answers will vary.

11a. perimeter = 28 meters, area = 48 square meters

11b. Possible answers:
1 × 48 rectangle (perimeter = 98 meters), 2 × 24 rectangle (perimeter = 52 meters), 3 × 16 rectangle (perimeter = 38 meters), 4 × 12 rectangle (perimeter = 32 meters)

11c. Answers will vary. For perimeter = 98 meters, many rectangles are possible: 2 × 47 (area = 94 square meters), 3 × 46 (area = 138 square meters), 4 × 45 (area = 180 square meters), etc. (As long as the dimensions add to 49 meters, the rectangle will have a perimeter of 98 meters.) For perimeter = 52 meters, the dimensions must add to 26 meters. For perimeter = 38 meters, the dimensions must add to 19 meters. For perimeter = 32 meters, the dimensions must add to 16 meters.

12. The dimensions are $1\frac{1}{2}$ inches by $2\frac{1}{2}$ inches, thus area = $3\frac{3}{4}$ square inches and perimeter = 8 inches.

13. The dimensions are $1\frac{1}{4}$ inches by 3 inches, thus area = $3\frac{3}{4}$ square inches and perimeter = $8\frac{1}{2}$ inches. (Some students might think one side is $1\frac{1}{3}$ inches. This is also reasonable and would make area = 4 square inches and perimeter = $8\frac{2}{3}$ inches.)

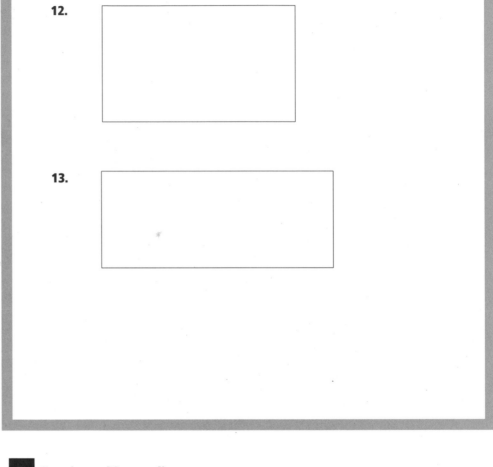

b. On grid paper, draw a rectangle with the same area as the one shown on the previous page, but a different perimeter. Label its dimensions, and give its perimeter.

c. On your grid paper, draw a rectangle with the same perimeter as the rectangle you just drew, but a different area. Label its dimensions, and give its area.

In 12 and 13, give the area, in square inches, and the perimeter, in inches, of the rectangle.

12.

13.

14. a.   Find the area and perimeter of the rectangle below.

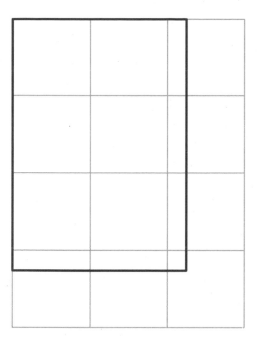

b.   On inch grid paper, draw a rectangle with the same perimeter as the rectangle shown, but with a different area. Label the rectangle with its length and width, and give its area.

14a.   area = $7\frac{15}{16}$ square inches, perimeter = 11 inches

14b.   Answers will vary. The sum of two adjacent sides must be 5.5 inches. Possible answer: a 2.5 inches by 3 inches rectangle; area = 7.5 square inches

Extensions

15a. $\frac{1}{4}$ meter or 0.25 meter

15b. rectangle; side lengths are $\frac{1}{4}$ meter, $\frac{1}{8}$ meter, $\frac{1}{4}$ meter, $\frac{1}{8}$ meter; perimeter = $\frac{3}{4}$ meter

15c. a rectangle; side lengths are $\frac{1}{4}$ meter, $\frac{3}{16}$ meter, $\frac{1}{4}$ meter, $\frac{3}{16}$ meter; perimeter = $\frac{7}{8}$ meter

15d. a rectangle; side lengths are $\frac{1}{4}$ meter, $\frac{7}{32}$ meter, $\frac{1}{4}$ meter, $\frac{7}{32}$ meter; perimeter = $\frac{15}{16}$ meter

15e. perimeter = $\frac{31}{32}$ meter

Extensions

15. Suppose a square sheet of paper has a perimeter of 1 meter.

a. What is the length of each side?

b. Suppose you folded the square sheet in half. What new shape would you have? What would the lengths of the shape's four sides be? What would the perimeter be?

c. Suppose you had folded over the top $\frac{1}{4}$ of the square. What new shape would you have? What would the lengths of the shape's four sides be? What would the perimeter be?

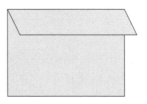

d. Suppose you had folded over only the top $\frac{1}{8}$ of the square. What new shape would you have? What would the lengths of the shape's four sides be? What would the perimeter be?

e. What would you predict for the perimeter of the shape you would get by folding over $\frac{1}{16}$ of the square?

Mathematical Reflections

In this investigation, you examined how the areas of shapes with the same perimeter could vary. First, you looked at rectangular pens with perimeters of 24 meters and decided which pens would give a dog the most room for running and for playing. Then you experimented with adding tiles to a pentomino, and you determined the smallest and the largest numbers of tiles you could add to the pentomino to make a shape with a perimeter of 18 units. These questions will help you summarize what you have learned:

1. Do all rectangles with the same perimeter have the same area? Explain your answer.

2. Of all rectangles with a given perimeter and whole-number side lengths, which rectangle has the smallest area?

3. Of all rectangles with a given perimeter and whole-number side lengths, which rectangle has the largest area?

Think about your answers to these questions, discuss your ideas with other students and your teacher, and then write a summary of your findings in your journal.

When you design the city park, how will these new ideas about perimeter and area help you? What things in a park would require information about area and perimeter? What areas might you want fencing around? Will you have sidewalks or paths in your park? You might want to start measuring some things like sidewalks and basketball courts now in preparation for designing the park. Remember to record in your journal all measurements that might help you with your project.

Possible Answers

1. no; Perimeter is the length around a shape. You can enclose different areas with the same length.

2. The longest, thinnest rectangle will have the smallest area. This is the rectangle with two sides of length 1 unit.

3. The rectangle that is the most like a square will have the greatest area.

4.1 • Fencing in Spaces

In this problem, students are asked to find all the rectangles with whole-number side lengths and a fixed perimeter of 24 units. This problem is more difficult than Problem 3.1, in which area was fixed. When students have completed this problem, they should be able to describe a pattern, rule, or formula for finding the perimeter of a rectangle and for finding the largest or smallest possible area for a rectangle of a fixed perimeter.

Launch

Read the introduction to the investigation with the class. Before students start designing dog pens, make sure they understand the mathematical context.

> In the last investigation, we found all the rectangles that could be made with an area of 12 square units and whole-number side lengths. Now I want you to think about all the rectangles that can be made with a perimeter of 12 units. This time, we are holding the perimeter fixed.
>
> Once you think you have an example, use your tiles and build your rectangle. Share your results with someone near you. Convince that person that you have built a rectangle with a perimeter of 12 units.
>
> Tell me what you built by giving me the dimensions (the lengths of the sides), the perimeter, and area for your rectangle.

On the board, record the length, width, and area of each rectangle students suggest. Continue collecting examples until all possibilities have been found. If you include reversals, there are five possibilities.

Length	Width	Perimeter	Area
1 unit	5 units	12 units	5 square units
2 units	4 units	12 units	8 square units
3 units	3 units	12 units	9 square units
4 units	2 units	12 units	8 square units
5 units	1 unit	12 units	5 square units

> How do we know we have found all the rectangles we can make with a perimeter of 12 units?

Your students may not be able to answer this question now. If they are struggling, ask them to continue to think about this question. We will return to it in the summary of Problem 4.1.

Read the problem with your class. Make sure students understand what they are to do.

> As you work on this problem, record your findings in a table similar to the one we used to find all the rectangles with a perimeter of 12 units.

Explore

Because working with constant perimeter is more difficult than working with constant area, you may want to have students work with a partner to find all possible rectangles. Each student should keep a record of the pair's findings.

As you circulate, you may notice that some students are frustrated with trying to find examples. Encourage them to try adding on or taking off more tiles so as to maintain a rectangle, or to try changing only one dimension at a time.

Summarize

You might begin the summary by collecting the data students recorded.

> Did anyone find a rectangular dog pen with a perimeter of 24 meters and an edge length of 1 meter? What is the width of that dog pen? What is the area? What does this dog pen look like?
>
> Did anyone find a rectangular dog pen with perimeter of 24 meters and an edge length of 2 meters? What is the width of that dog pen? What is the area? What does this dog pen look like?

Continue with this line of questioning until all possible rectangles have been given.

Length	Width	Perimeter	Area	
1 meter	11 meters	24 meters	11 square meters	
2 meters	10 meters	24 meters	20 square meters	
3 meters	9 meters	24 meters	27 square meters	
4 meters	8 meters	24 meters	32 square meters	
5 meters	7 meters	24 meters	35 square meters	
6 meters	6 meters	24 meters	36 square meters	
7 meters	5 meters	24 meters	35 square meters	
8 meters	4 meters	24 meters	32 square meters	
9 meters	3 meters	24 meters	27 square meters	
10 meters	2 meters	24 meters	20 square meters	
11 meters	1 meter	24 meters	11 square meters	

Look at the table we have generated. What patterns do you notice? Explain why each pattern you see makes sense.

Here are some patterns students have noticed.

- Rosa noticed that the area of each rectangle is the length times the width. (This verifies the pattern noticed in the last investigation.)

- Ali said that as one side gets bigger, the other gets smaller. (You have a total of 24 units for perimeter; if you increase the number of units on one side, you must decrease the number of units on the other side.)

- Joel noticed that the numbers are in order from 1 to 11 and from 11 to 1.

- Letty discovered that the sum of the length and the width is half the total perimeter. (A rectangle has two lengths and two widths, so the sum of one length and one width equals half the perimeter.)

Can anyone describe a pattern or formula for finding the perimeter of a rectangle?

After a student describes a way to find the perimeter, ask if anyone thought about it in a different way. Most students will give the rule in words. You may want to help them translate their words to symbolic form. In most classes, students will describe perimeter as the sum of the four sides of a rectangle:

perimeter = length + width + length + width   or $P = l + w + l + w$

Some students may find the sum of the length and width and then double the answer:

perimeter = (length + width) × 2   or $P = (l + w) \times 2$

Other students may add two lengths to two widths:

perimeter = 2 × length + 2 × width   or $P = 2 \times l + 2 \times w$

Have students test their rules by giving them the length and width of a rectangle and having them find the perimeter.

Use the follow-up questions to discuss which rectangles have smaller areas and which rectangles have larger areas.

4.2 • Adding Tiles to Pentominos

In this problem, students continue to investigate fixed perimeter and changing area; however, they are no longer restricted to rectangles. They now consider how adding tiles to a pentomino changes the perimeter of the figure. They explore the patterns of change that occur as they add tiles that touch existing tiles on one, two, or three sides.

Launch

Draw the following pentomino on the board, or display Transparency 4.2, and have students construct the pentomino with their tiles.

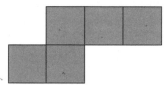

What is the area of this figure? (*5 square units*) What is the perimeter? (*12 units*)

Tell students they must keep these five tiles in this arrangement as part of any figure they construct for Problem 4.2. If the tiles students are using come in more than one color, you might suggest that they use one color for the pentomino and another color for the tiles they add.

Explore

This is a nice problem for students to do with a partner, but have each student keep a record of the results.

If any students seem stuck on how to approach the follow-up, ask how the perimeter of the figure changes when they add a tile so that it touches the pentomino on one side. Then, ask how the perimeter changes when they add a tile so that it touches the pentomino on two sides.

Summarize

Start the summary by discussing part B.

> What is the smallest number of tiles you can add to the pentomino to get a perimeter of 18 units? (*3*) Show us your arrangement on the board.

There are several possibilities. Have two or three students show different arrangements. Here is one possibility.

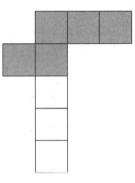

> Where should you add the three tiles to get the perimeter to increase as quickly as possible? (*on an edge, so that only one side of each new tile touches any other tile*)

> What is the largest number of tiles you can add to get a perimeter of 18 units? Did anyone add a greater number of tiles and still keep the perimeter 18 units? What does the figure you got with the maximum area and a perimeter of 18 units look like?

The largest number of tiles that can be added is 15. This maximum area is a 4×5 rectangle. Here is one possible arrangement of the tiles.

Now discuss the follow-up question.

How did adding tiles change the perimeter?

Students should be able to tell you what happens if a tile is added so that it touches exactly one, two, or three other tiles. There are three possible ways to add a tile:

■ You can add a tile so that it touches one edge of the figure. This adds three exposed edges and eliminates one, *increasing the perimeter by 2 units*.

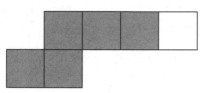

■ You can add a tile so that it touches two tiles. This adds two exposed edges and eliminates two, *leaving the perimeter unchanged*.

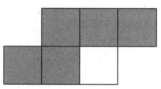

■ You can slip a tile into a space surrounded by three tiles. This adds one exposed edge and eliminates three, *decreasing the perimeter by 2 units*.

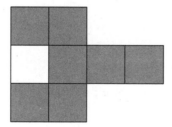

Additional Answers

Answers to Problem 4.2

A. Answers will vary. Possible arrangements:

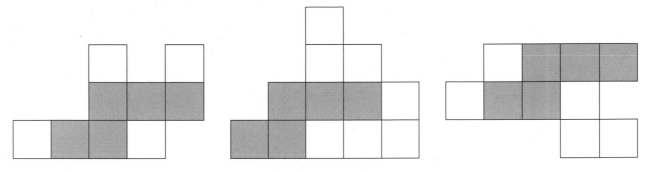

B. 3; Possible arrangements (each of the three tiles must touch only one edge as they are added):

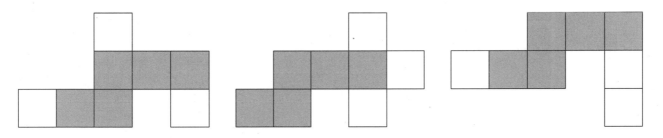

C. 15; Possible arrangements (each figure must enclose the pentomino in a 4 × 5 rectangle):

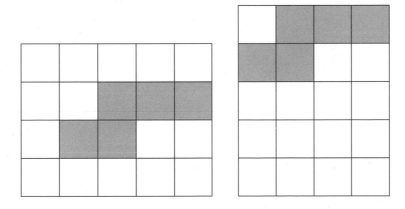

Measuring Parallelograms

In this investigation, students deepen their understanding of area and perimeter by finding areas and perimeters of parallelograms. In Problem 5.1, Finding Measures of Parallelograms, students count and estimate to find areas of parallelograms. In Problem 5.2, Designing Parallelograms Under Constraints, students draw parallelograms satisfying given restrictions. Problem 5.3, Rearranging Parallelograms, asks students to make one cut through a parallelogram so that the pieces can be rearranged to form a rectangle. The hands-on constructions in these problems allow students to tackle a new task (finding the area of a parallelogram) by relating it to something they can already do (finding the area of rectangle).

As students work through the problems, ask questions to further their understanding of the relationships between area and perimeter of rectangles and parallelograms. Do a parallelogram and a rectangle with the same perimeter always have the same area? If the area of a parallelogram and a rectangle are the same, do they necessarily have the same perimeter?

Mathematical and Problem-Solving Goals

- **To discover relationships between parallelograms and rectangles**

- **To use relationships between rectangles and parallelograms to develop techniques or formulas for finding areas and perimeters of parallelograms**

- **To apply techniques for finding areas and perimeters of rectangles and parallelograms to a variety of problem situations**

Materials		
Problem	For students	For the teacher
All	Calculators	Transparencies 5.1 to 5.3 (optional), transparency of centimeter grid paper (optional)
5.1	Labsheet 5.1	
5.2	Centimeter grid paper (provided as a blackline master)	
5.3	Centimeter grid paper (provided as a blackline master), centimeter rulers, scissors	

Student Pages 46–55   Teaching the Investigation 55a–55g

Finding Measures of Parallelograms

Launch

- Review the introduction to the investigation and read Problem 5.1.

Explore

- Have students work in pairs to find the areas of the seven parallelograms.

Summarize

- As a class, record students' area measurements.

- Discuss students' strategies for determining the area of a parallelogram.

Measuring Parallelograms

You have found areas and perimeters of both rectangular and nonrectangular shapes. When a rectangle is displayed on a grid, you can find the area by counting the number of squares enclosed by the rectangle. You may have found that, once you counted the grid squares in one row, you could multiply by the number of rows to find the total number of squares in the rectangle. In other words, you can find the area of a rectangle by multiplying the length by the width.

For example, in this rectangle there are 5 squares in the first row and 7 rows in all. The area of the rectangle is $5 \times 7 = 35$ square units.

For a nonrectangular figure, you found that you could estimate the area by covering the figure with a grid and counting square units. In the next two investigations, you will find shortcuts for calculating areas of some special figures, including parallelograms. But don't forget that you can always cover a figure with a grid and count squares to find area.

5.1 Finding Measures of Parallelograms

On the next page are seven parallelograms drawn on a grid. Some of the parallelograms are not covered by whole squares. Even the two rectangles have sides that are not whole numbers of units long.

Assignment Choices

ACE question 12 and unassigned choices from earlier problems

Problem 5.1

For parallelograms A–G, find the area and explain how you found it.

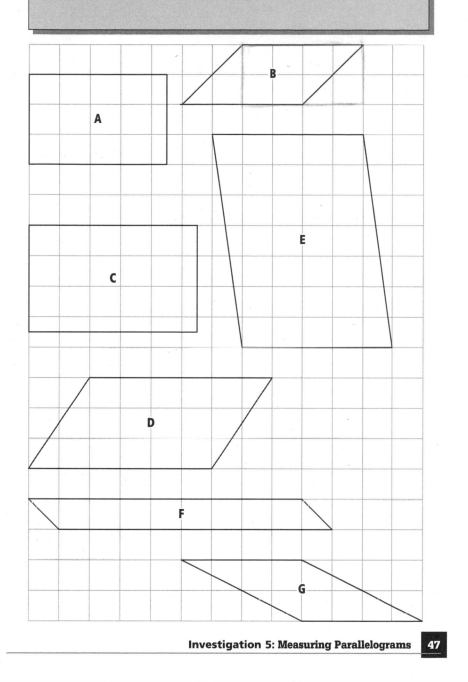

Answers to Problem 5.1

A. $13\frac{1}{2}$ square units; There are 12 whole squares and 3 half squares.

B. 8 square units; Cut off a triangle. Move it to the other side to make a 2 × 4 rectangle.

C. $19\frac{1}{4}$ square units; There are 15 whole squares, 8 half squares, and 1 fourth square.

D. 18 square units; Take a 3 × 8 rectangle and subtract a 2 × 3 rectangle.

E. 35 square units; There are 28 whole squares and a triangle on each side. Each triangle is half of a 1 × 7 rectangle, or $3\frac{1}{2}$ square units. Together the triangles are 7 square units. The total area is 28 + 7, or 35, square units.

F. 9 square units; There are 8 whole squares and 2 half squares.

G. 8 square units; Make a vertical cut in the middle and slide the pieces together to make a 4 × 2 rectangle.

At a Glance

**Grouping:
Pairs**

Launch

- Discuss what the base and height of a parallelogram are.

- Verify that students understand how to measure the base and height of a parallelogram.

Explore

- Have students work in pairs to draw parallelograms that meet the given constraints.

- Pose additional questions for students who finish early. (*optional*)

Summarize

- As a class, discuss which kinds of constraints are easy and which are difficult.

- Have students share their answers, their strategies for determining area of a parallelogram, and shortcuts they found.

■ **Problem 5.1 Follow-Up**

Find the area and the perimeter of this parallelogram. Explain your reasoning.

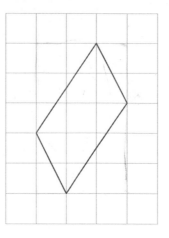

5.2 **Designing Parallelograms Under Constraints**

Parallelograms are often described by giving their **base** and **height**. The drawings illustrate the meanings of these terms.

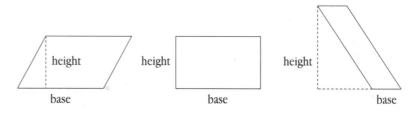

You can think of the height as the distance a rock would fall if you dropped it from a point at the top of a parallelogram down to the line that the base is on. In the first parallelogram, if we dropped the rock from the upper-left corner, it would fall inside the parallelogram. In the second parallelogram (a rectangle), the rock could fall along one of the sides. In the third parallelogram, if we dropped the rock from the upper-left corner, it would fall outside the parallelogram.

Assignment Choices

ACE questions 8, 15, and unassigned choices from earlier problems

Answer to Problem 5.1 Follow-Up

The area is 7 square units. You can get this by surrounding the figure with a 3 × 5 rectangle. Find the area of the rectangle and then subtract the areas of the four triangles on the corners. This gives 15 − (3 + 1 + 3 + 1), or 7, square units.

In the next problem, you will draw parallelograms that meet given requirements, or *constraints*. Sometimes you will be able to draw more than one parallelogram that satisfies the constraints.

Problem 5.2

In A–E, make your drawings on centimeter grid paper. Note that cm is the abbreviation for centimeters, and cm² is the abbreviation for square centimeters.

A. Draw a rectangle with an area of 18 cm². Then, try to draw a different rectangle with an area of 18 cm². Do the rectangles have the same perimeter? If you couldn't draw a different rectangle, explain why.

B. Draw a rectangle with the dimensions 3 cm by 8 cm. Then, try to draw a different rectangle with these same dimensions. Do the rectangles have the same area? If you couldn't draw a different rectangle, explain why.

C. Draw a parallelogram with a base of 7 cm and a height of 4 cm. Then, try to draw a different parallelogram with these same dimensions. Do the parallelograms have the same area? If you couldn't draw a different parallelogram, explain why.

D. Draw a parallelogram with all side lengths equal to 6 cm. Then, try to draw a different parallelogram with all side lengths equal to 6 cm. Do the parallelograms have the same area? If you couldn't draw a different parallelogram, explain why.

E. Draw a parallelogram with an area of 30 cm². Then, try to draw a different parallelogram with the same area. Do the parallelograms have the same perimeter? If you couldn't draw a different parallelogram, explain why.

■ Problem 5.2 Follow-Up

1. Summarize what you have discovered from making parallelograms that fit given constraints. Include your feelings about what kinds of constraints make designing a parallelogram easy and what kinds of constraints make designing a parallelogram difficult.

2. Have you discovered any shortcuts for finding areas of parallelograms? If so, describe them.

Answers to Problem 5.2

See page 55f.

Answers to Problem 5.2 Follow-Up

1. Answers will vary. Most likely students will find it easiest to construct a rectangle when the dimensions are given, and a parallelogram when the base and height are given. Many students probably find it difficult to construct a parallelogram with a fixed area.

2. Answers will vary. Some students may have discovered the formula for area of a parallelogram, *area = base × height*.

5.3 Rearranging Parallelograms

Rearranging Parallelograms

As you have probably discovered in your work, it would be useful to develop some easy ways to find perimeters and areas of common polygons without having to cover them with a grid and count squares. Let's do some exploring...

Problem 5.3

Draw two different nonrectangular parallelograms on a sheet of grid paper, and cut them out. Cut one of your parallelograms into two pieces so that the pieces can be reassembled to form a rectangle. Do the same for the second parallelogram. Use one of your parallelograms to complete parts A–C.

A. Record the base, height, perimeter, and area of the original parallelogram.

B. Record the length, width, perimeter, and area of the rectangle you made from the parallelogram pieces.

C. What relationships do you see between the measures for the rectangle and the measures for the parallelogram from which it was made?

■ **Problem 5.3 Follow-Up**

Use what you have learned to find the area and perimeter of this parallelogram.

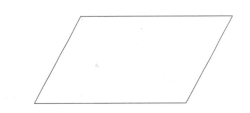

At a Glance

**Grouping:
Individuals**

Launch

■ As a class, discuss the strategies students have used so far in finding areas and perimeters of parallelograms.

■ When students are ready, let them start drawing and cutting parallelograms.

Explore

■ After students have experimented, have them choose one parallelogram to use in the problem.

Summarize

■ Collect students' results in a table.

■ Have students check any unreasonable measurements and then look for patterns.

■ Help students make the connection between length and width of a rectangle and base and height of a parallelogram.

Assignment Choices

ACE questions 1–7, 9–11, 13, 14, 16, and unassigned choices from earlier problems

Answers to Problem 5.3

A. Answers will vary.

B. Answers will vary, but length and width should equal base and height from part A, and area should equal area from part A.

C. Possible answer: The base of the parallelogram turned into the length of the rectangle, the height of the parallelogram turned into the width of the rectangle, and the area stayed the same.

Answers to Problem 5.3 Follow-Up

area = 14 cm^2 to 14.5 cm^2, perimeter = 16.4 cm to 16.6 cm

As you work on these ACE questions, use your calculator whenever you need it.

Applications

In 1–7, find the area and perimeter of the polygon, and write a brief explanation of your reasoning for 2, 6, and 7.

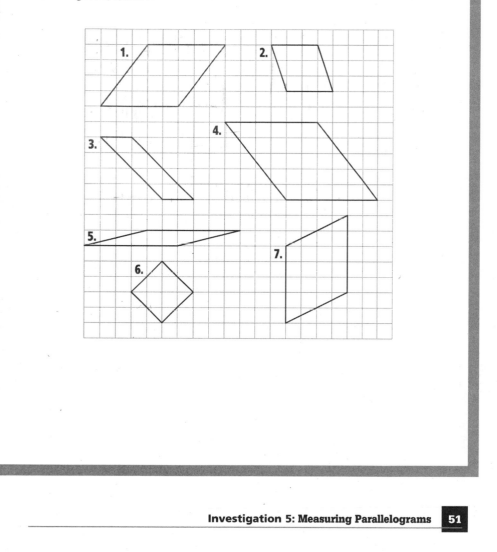

Answers

Applications

1. area = 20 square units (base = 5, height = 4), perimeter = about 25 units (dimensions are 5 by about 5)

2. area = 9 square units (base = 3, height = 3), perimeter = about 12.5 units (dimensions are 3 by about 3.25)

3. area = 8 square units (base = 2, height = 4), perimeter = about 15 units (dimensions are 2 by about 5.5)

4. area = 30 square units (base = 6, height = 5), perimeter = about 25 units (dimensions are 6 by about 6.5)

5. area = 6 square units (base = 6, height = 1), perimeter = about 20 units (dimensions are 6 by about 4)

6. See page 55f.

7. area = 20 square units (base = 5, height = 4), perimeter = about 19 units (dimensions are 5 by about 4.5)

8a. area = 20 square units for each parallelogram

8b. Possible answers: The area is the same for each parallelogram even though the perimeters are different. As you move the top edge further to the right, the perimeter increases while the area remains the same.

8c. Possible answer: Because they all have the same area, base, and height.

9. area = 6 cm²,
perimeter = 10.48 cm

10. area = 6 cm²,
perimeter = 16.48 cm

11. area = 16 cm²,
perimeter = 16.24 cm

8. Below is a *family* of parallelograms.

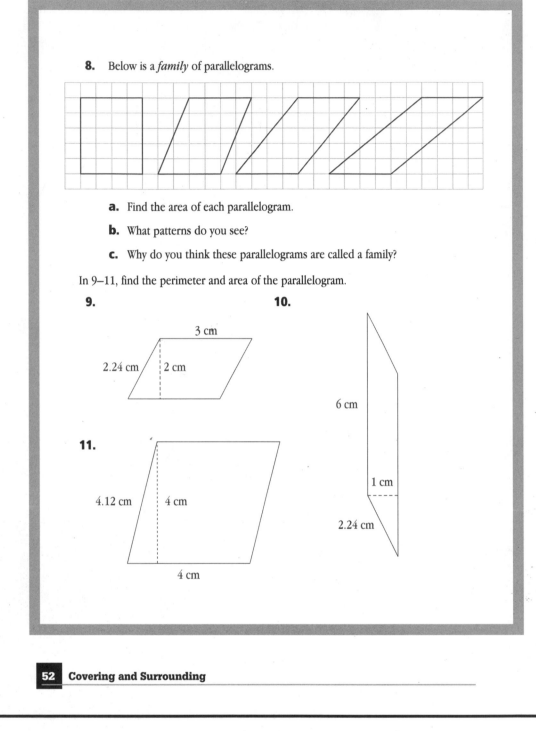

a. Find the area of each parallelogram.

b. What patterns do you see?

c. Why do you think these parallelograms are called a family?

In 9–11, find the perimeter and area of the parallelogram.

9.

3 cm

2.24 cm   2 cm

10.

6 cm

1 cm

2.24 cm

11.

4.12 cm   4 cm

4 cm

Connections

12. In *Shapes and Designs*, you found that if you make a rectangle out of Polystrips and press on the corners, the rectangle tilts out of a shape into a different parallelogram.

a. How will the sides, angles, area, and perimeter of the new parallelogram compare to the original rectangle?

b. What relations among the sides and angles of rectangles are also true of parallelograms?

13. In *Shapes and Designs*, you learned about shapes that can tile a flat surface.

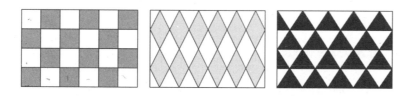

a. The floor plan on the following page is to be tiled with rectangular tiles like the one shown. Use your understanding of area and perimeter to calculate the number of tiles needed to cover the floor. Explain your reasoning.

b. How would your reasoning change if you were to use nonrectangular parallelograms as tiles?

Connections

12a. Possible answer: The side lengths will remain the same, so the perimeter remains the same. The angles change, but the sum of two adjacent angles is always 180°. The area gets smaller as the parallelogram tilts further.

12b. Possible answer: Opposite sides are always equal. Adjacent angles always add to 180°, and the sum of the four angles is 360°.

13a. It would take 29 tiles to cover the floor. Possible explanation: I figured out how many tiles would fit in the figure by measuring side lengths and fitting the tiles into the floor plan.

13b. Possible answer: If the tiles had the same area as the rectangular tiles, you would need the same number of tiles, but you would need to cut up some of the tiles and rearrange the pieces to cover the floor. If the tiles did not have the same area as the rectangular tiles, you would need to find the area of the room and the area of a tile and then divide the area of the room by the area of a tile to find out how many tiles you would need to cover the floor.

14. Answers will vary. The base of the parallelogram times the height must equal 24.

Extensions

15. See page 55g.

16. See page 55g.

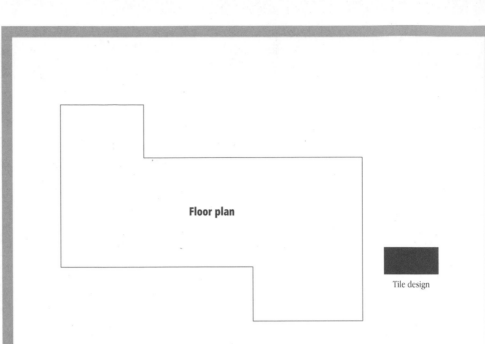

Floor plan

Tile design

14. Suppose you had a plot of land and you wanted to use what you have learned in this unit to design a garden. Design a parallelogram-shaped flower bed with an area of 24 square feet.

Extensions

15. Draw a parallelogram with a base of 6 centimeters and an area of 30 square centimeters. If possible, draw a second parallelogram with the same dimensions.

16. Design a rectangle with an area of 9 square centimeters. Make two sides a whole-number length, and two sides a length that is not a whole number. If possible, draw a second rectangle under these same constraints.

Mathematical Reflections

In this investigation, you invented strategies for finding areas and perimeters of parallelograms. These questions will help you summarize what you have learned:

1 Describe at least one efficient way to find the area of a parallelogram. Explain why it works.

2 Describe at least one efficient way to find the perimeter of a parallelogram. Explain why it works.

Think about your answers to these questions, discuss your ideas with other students and your teacher, and then write a summary of your findings in your journal.

How might your new knowledge about parallelograms help you in your park design? Have you thought about designing picnic areas or gardens in the shape of a parallelogram?

Possible Answers

1. The most efficient way to find the area of a parallelogram that is a rectangle is to multiply the length and width. The most efficient way to find the area of a parallelogram that is not a rectangle is to multiply the length of one of its sides (call this the base) by the perpendicular distance between that side and the opposite side (call this the height). You can see that this works by cutting and rearranging the parallelogram to form a rectangle (see below left).

The dimensions of the rectangle are the same as the base and height of the original parallelogram. You have changed the perimeter but not the area.

2. To find the perimeter of any parallelogram, you just add the lengths of its four sides. A shortcut is to add two adjacent side lengths and double the amount. This works because *perimeter* is the distance around a figure, so it is the sum of the side lengths of that figure.

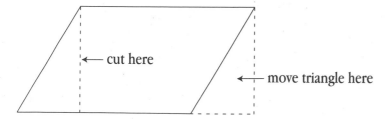

cut here

move triangle here

5.1 • Finding Measures of Parallelograms

This problem asks students to find the areas of two rectangles and five nonrectangular parallelograms. The purpose of this activity is to have students *develop and employ reasonable strategies* for finding the areas of these figures (not to use the formula for area of a parallelogram): counting, estimating, and talking about ways to deal with parts of grid squares.

Launch

As a class, read the introduction to the investigation, the introduction to the problem, and the problem. Give each student a copy of Labsheet 5.1. Because students have already estimated areas of nonrectangular shapes, they should have some strategies for working with these figures. Remind students that they need to be able to explain how they found each area.

Explore

Have students work in pairs to find the areas of the figures. As you circulate, remind them to record their findings and to describe their strategies.

Summarize

Ask students for the measures they found for each figure, and record their answers on the board. Continue to collect answers (even if you have several different areas proposed for the same figure) until all the different answers that groups found are recorded.

Figure	Area
A	13.5 square units
B	8 square units
C	19.25 square units
D	18 square units
E	35 square units
F	9 square units
G	8 square units

Next, focus the class's attention on figure A, and point to one of the given answers.

> Explain how you found this area measure for figure A. Is that measure reasonable? Did anyone find the area using a different method?

If the student did not find the area by multiplying length and width, ask:

> Would you get the same answer if you multiplied the length, $4\frac{1}{2}$, by the width, 3? What is 3 groups of $4\frac{1}{2}$ equal to?

Move to figure C, the second rectangle.

> Explain how you found your area measure for figure C.

In most classes, students will have found the areas of the figures by counting, even for the two rectangles. This gives you a good opportunity to encourage them to try the rule for the area of a rectangle on figures that have side lengths that are small, "friendly" fractions or decimals. This gives students a chance to think about what happens when rational numbers are added and multiplied.

> Now, explain how you found the area measure for figure B. Is that measure reasonable? Did anyone find the area using a different method? What are the measures of the edges of this parallelogram?

You may need to talk about how to measure the sides of parallelograms that are not aligned with the grid. They can be measured using the edge of a sheet of grid paper.

> If we multiply the measures of the two edges together—as we do for rectangles—do we get the same number that we agreed was the area of figure B?

The agreed-upon area for figure B should be 8 square units. The lengths of the edges of the parallelogram should be 4 units and approximately 3 units. Multiplying these gives 12 square units, not 8. This observation should start your students questioning the idea of multiplying the two side lengths to find the area of parallelograms.

This discussion can be repeated for the remaining parallelograms until all areas are found. Counting squares to verify areas should be encouraged at this point.

5.2 • Designing Parallelograms Under Constraints

In this activity, students are asked to construct rectangles and parallelograms with certain given measurements. In each case, they are asked whether they can draw a different rectangle or parallelogram with the same constraints and to determine whether the area or perimeter of the two figures differ.

Launch

Discuss the overview of base and height on page 48 of the student edition. The *height* of a parallelogram is the perpendicular distance from one side to the opposite side. Explain to students that they are going to construct rectangles and parallelograms satisfying measurements that are given. Students may be given edge lengths, height, or area.

Read part C of the problem aloud. Ask students if they understand what is meant by "a height of 4 cm." If they don't, refer them to figure B in Problem 5.1. Review with them that the lengths of the edges are 4 and about 3. Demonstrate that the height is 2 units: because of the orientation of this parallelogram, it is easy to measure the vertical distance between the two sides of 4 units. We could measure the perpendicular distance between the two shorter sides, but it would require measuring with a ruler. If students need more practice, have them identify the height of the other parallelograms in Problem 5.1.

Choose a student to come to the overhead projector and draw a parallelogram with base 7 cm and height 4 cm on a centimeter grid. When the class agrees this was done successfully, have students work in pairs on the rest of the problem.

Have several sheets of grid paper available; students will make mistakes. To save time and materials, you might suggest that they cross out figures that don't meet the requirements rather than throwing away their paper.

Explore

Each student should make his or her own drawings. Pairs can discuss how to approach each part, then check each other's drawings. As you circulate, remind students to label their drawings so that they are easy to refer to during the summary.

Pairs that finish early can work on the follow-up questions, and you may want to pose additional questions for them.

> Draw three rectangles, each with an area of 18 square units and with at least one edge that is not a whole-number length.

> Can you construct a rectangle with an area of 18 square units and a perimeter larger than the perimeter of the 1 × 18 rectangle or smaller than the perimeter of the 3 × 6 rectangle?

Summarize

Start the summary by discussing the first follow-up question, which asks students what they have found from making these designs.

> What kinds of constraints make drawing a figure easy? What kinds of constraints make drawing a figure difficult?

If a student identifies a certain type of information as difficult, ask the other students whether they came up with strategies for drawing parallelograms under that kind of constraint.

> Were there any questions for which you could make only one figure that fits the constraints?

If students say no, ask them to share what they found for part B. If they give two different rectangles, the second is probably a different orientation of the first. By now most of your students should agree that these rectangles are really the same: they have the same dimensions, area, and perimeter.

Continue to have students share their responses to the parts of the problem. After one student gives an answer, ask if anyone has a different answer. You want students to see the variety of responses possible for parts A, C, D, and E. They should understand that fixing the length of the sides or the height of a nonrectangular parallelogram does not limit the figure to one shape as it does for rectangles. You also want them to notice that—if a group of parallelograms has sides of the same length—the parallelogram with sides that are the most "slanted" has the smallest area.

> Did you discover any shortcuts for finding the area of a parallelogram?

If someone knows and uses the formula, ask him or her to explain why it works. If the student cannot explain, ask the rest of the class whether they agree with the formula and whether anyone can explain why it makes sense. It is fine if students have not noticed any shortcuts. This question is addressed in the next problem.

5.3 • Rearranging Parallelograms

In this problem, students discover that a parallelogram can be cut and the pieces rearranged to form a rectangle with same area as the original parallelogram. The length and width of the rectangle will be the same as the base and height of the parallelogram. Since the area of a rectangle can be found by multiplying its length by its width, the area of the parallelogram can be found by multiplying its base by its height.

Launch

Ask students to recall the work they have done in finding the perimeters and areas of parallelograms.

> In the problems we have done so far, how have we found perimeters of parallelograms that were not rectangles?

Finding the perimeter of a nonrectangular parallelogram is a bit more difficult than finding the perimeter of a rectangle, because we have to measure a side that does not align with the grid. Yet, once that side is measured, we can find the perimeter in the same way we do for a rectangle: add the four edge lengths or add the lengths of two adjacent edges (two edges that touch) and double the sum.

> How did we find areas of parallelograms that were not rectangles?

Finding the area of a nonrectangular parallelogram is more difficult than finding the area of a rectangle. For the most part, we have counted and estimated. Multiplying two edge lengths, as we do for a rectangle, does not give us the area.

> For large parallelograms, counting and estimating can be tedious. Today we want to look for a more efficient way for finding the area of a parallelogram.

Read Problem 5.3 with your students. When you feel they understand what to do, let them start drawing and cutting parallelograms.

Explore

Students should make and cut their own parallelograms but can work with partners to share their results. As you visit with students, make sure they are constructing nonrectangular parallelograms that are large enough to work with easily. After they have done some experimenting, tell them to choose a parallelogram and use it to complete the problem.

When students complete the problem, ask them to work on the follow-up questions.

Summarize

Create a table with the following column heads on the board.

Parallelogram					Rectangle			
Base	Side length adjacent to base	Height	Perimeter	Area	Length	Width	Perimeter	Area

Have students fill in their results for each category. After several students have recorded their results, have the class examine the table to see whether any measurements seem unreasonable. After discussing, remeasuring, and correcting those measurements, ask students to look for patterns.

> What measures of the parallelogram and the rectangle made by cutting and rearranging the parallelogram are the same? *(the length of one of the edges, and the area)* What measures are different? *(the length of the other edge, and the perimeter)*

> What measurements did you need to make to find the perimeter of the parallelograms? Explain why. *(the lengths of the outside edges, because perimeter is the total length of the outside edges)*

> What measurements could you use to calculate the area of a parallelogram so that you don't have to count and estimate? *(the base and the height)*

> How do those measurements relate to the measures of the rectangle you made from the parallelogram? *(The base and height of the parallelogram are the same as the length and width of the rectangle.)*

Ask students to summarize the patterns they have noticed and discussed. Here are some patterns students have noticed:

- Kara noticed that the height of a rectangle is the same as one of its edges. This is not always true for a parallelogram.

- Everett said that you find the perimeter for parallelograms and rectangles in the same way, by adding the lengths of all the sides.

- Molly noticed that the areas for the parallelogram and the rectangle made from the parallelogram are the same, but the perimeters are different.

- Caleb said that for parallelograms, multiplying the two side lengths does not give the area, but multiplying the base by the height does give the area.

- Nikki observed that if two parallelograms have the same perimeter, the parallelogram with the smaller height has the smaller area.

If a rule for the area of a parallelogram is suggested by a student (*area = base × height*), have students test whether it works for the parallelograms in Problem 5.1. If no one suggests a rule or pattern, mention that you noticed this pattern, and ask students whether it always holds true.

Conclude by discussing the follow-up, which asks students to find the area and perimeter of a parallelogram that is not drawn on a grid.

> What measurements must you have to calculate the area of this parallelogram? *(base and height)* What are the base and height of this parallelogram? *(The base is 5 centimeters; the height is between 2.8 and 2.9 centimeters.)*

> What is the area of the parallelogram? *(between 14 and 14.5 square centimeters)* How did you find that? *(by multiplying base by height)*

How can we test to see whether the area we calculated is reasonable? *(We can a place a transparent centimeter grid over the figure and count the number of squares that are inside the parallelogram.)*

What measurements would we need to find the perimeter? *(the lengths of the base and one of the sides that it touches)* What are the lengths of the base and adjacent side? *(The base is 5 centimeters; the adjacent side is between 3.2 and 3.3 centimeters.)*

How do you find the perimeter of a parallelogram? *(Add the lengths of two touching sides and double the sum.)* What is the perimeter of this parallelogram? *(between 16.4 and 16.6 centimeters)*

Additional Answers

Answers to Problem 5.2

A. Drawings will vary. The most common drawings will be 1×18, 2×9, and 3×6 rectangles. The rectangles do not have the same perimeter.

B. It is not possible to draw two different rectangles. Some students may draw the same rectangle twice with different orientations.

C. Drawings will vary. All the parallelograms will have an area of 28 cm². A geoboard is an excellent tool for demonstrating that you can keep the same base and height, but move the side parallel to the base to get different parallelograms with the same area.

D. Drawings will vary. The areas of the parallelograms can vary from 0 to 36 cm².

E. Drawings will vary. The base times the height of all the parallelograms will be 30 cm². The perimeters of the parallelograms will vary.

ACE Answers

Applications

6. area = 8 square units, perimeter = about 11.2 units (dimensions are about 2.8 by about 2.8)

For the Teacher: Explaining ACE Question 6

The area of this square can be found easily. The length of the sides, from the Pythagorean Theorem, are $\sqrt{8} = 2.8284271$. We don't expect students will know this, but some families who help their children may offer this as an answer. Some students may say that the length of the sides is 3 units and thus the perimeter is 12 units. Although this is close, you will want to discuss why it is not possible for the length to be 3 units (if it were, the area would be 9 square units, and they can easily see from the drawing that this is not the case).

Extensions

15. Answers will vary. Some possibilities:

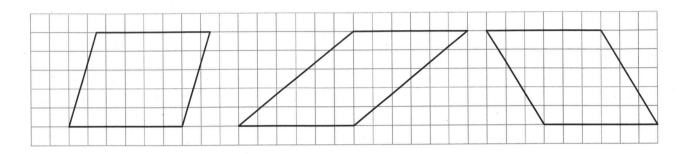

16. There are an infinite number of possible answers. Here are three:

Measuring Triangles

In this investigation, students deepen their understanding of area and perimeter by finding areas and perimeters of triangles. In Problem 6.1, Finding Measures of Triangles, students count and estimate to find areas of triangles. Problem 6.2, Designing Triangles Under Constraints, asks students to draw triangles satisfying certain restrictions. Problem 6.3, Making Parallelograms from Triangles, asks students to piece together two copies of a triangle to form a parallelogram and to cut a parallelogram into two triangles of the same size and shape. The hands-on constructions in these problems allow students to tackle a new task (finding the area of a triangle) by relating it to something they can already do (finding the area of a parallelogram).

Mathematical and Problem-Solving Goals

- *To find relationships between triangles and parallelograms*

- *To use the relationships between rectangles and parallelograms and between parallelograms and triangles to develop techniques for finding areas and perimeters of triangles*

- *To apply techniques for finding areas and perimeters of rectangles, parallelograms, and triangles to a variety of problem situations*

Materials		
Problem	**For students**	**For the teacher**
All	Calculators	Transparencies 6.1 to 6.3 (optional), transparency of centimeter grid paper (optional; provided as a blackline master)
6.1	Labsheet 6.1	
6.2	Centimeter grid paper (provided as a blackline master)	
6.3	Centimeter grid paper, scissors, centimeter rulers, tape, inch grid paper (optional), construction paper (optional)	

6.1

Finding Measures of Triangles

Launch

- Relate this problem to the work students did with parallelograms in Problem 5.1.

- Make sure the class understands what they are to do.

Explore

- Have students work in pairs to find perimeters and areas of the eight triangles.

- As you circulate, encourage students to look for shortcuts.

Summarize

- As a class, record students' measurements.

- Demonstrate how a right triangle and a rectangle are related.

INVESTIGATION 6

Measuring Triangles

You can always find the area of a figure by overlaying a grid and counting squares, but you probably realize that this can be very time-consuming. In Investigation 5, you discovered a shortcut for finding the area of a parallelogram without counting squares. In this investigation, you will estimate areas of triangles and look for patterns that might help you discover a shortcut for finding the area of a triangle.

6.1 Finding Measures of Triangles

On the next page are eight triangles drawn on a grid. The triangles are not covered by whole numbers of unit squares.

> **Problem 6.1**
>
> For triangles A–H on page 57, find the area and perimeter and explain how you found them.

■ **Problem 6.1 Follow-Up**

Find the area and perimeter of this triangle. Explain your reasoning.

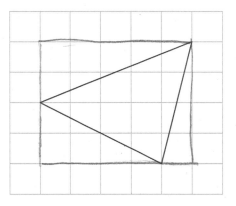

Assignment Choices

Unassigned choices from earlier problems

Answers to Problem 6.1

A. area = 12 square units, perimeter = about 17 units

B. area = 35 square units, perimeter = about 29 units

C. area = 12 square units, perimeter = about 19.5 units

D. area = 27 square units, perimeter = about 24 units

E. area = 16 square units, perimeter = about 19.5 units

F. area = 30 square units, perimeter = about 26.5 units

G. area = about 25.5 square units, perimeter = about 24.5 units

H. area = 21 square units, perimeter = about 21 units

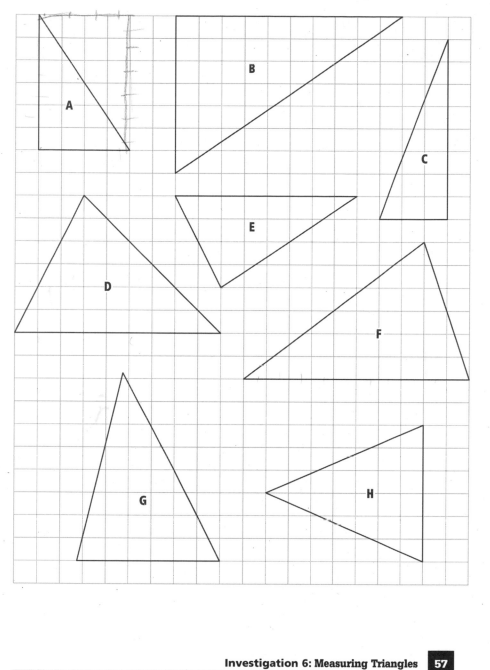

Answers to Problem 6.1 Follow-Up

The area is 9. You can find this by surrounding the triangle with a 4 × 5 rectangle. This forms three right triangles around the original triangle with areas of 5, 4,
and 2.

To find the area of the original triangle, subtract the
areas of these three right triangles from the area of the
rectangle. This gives 20 − (5 + 4 + 2), or 9, square units.
The perimeter is 14.2 square units. You can find this by
measuring the sides with a strip of grid paper, or, since
the grid is a centimeter grid, by using a centimeter ruler.

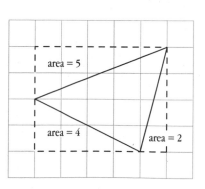

6.2

Designing Triangles Under Constraints

At a Glance

Grouping:
Pairs

Launch

- Discuss how to find the base and height of a triangle.

- Verify that students understand how to measure base and height of a triangle.

Explore

- Have students work in pairs to draw triangles that meet the given constraints.

- Have pairs who finish early work on the follow-up questions.

Summarize

- As a class, discuss which kinds of constraints are easy and which are difficult.

- Have students share their answers, their strategies for determining the area of a triangle, and shortcuts they found.

As with parallelograms, triangles are often described by giving their base and height. The drawings below illustrate what these terms mean.

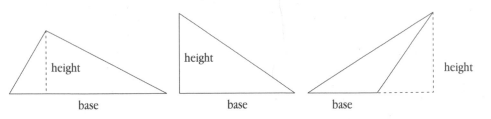

You can think of the height of a triangle as the distance a rock would fall if you dropped it from the top vertex of the triangle down to the line that the base is on. In the first triangle, the height falls inside the triangle. In the second triangle, the height is one of the sides. In the third triangle, the height falls outside the triangle.

In this problem, you will try to draw triangles that meet given constraints.

Problem 6.2

In A–D, make your drawings on centimeter grid paper. Remember that cm is the abbreviation for centimeters, and cm² is the abbreviation for square centimeters.

A. Draw a triangle with a base of 5 cm and a height of 6 cm. Then, try to draw a different triangle with these same dimensions. Do the triangles have the same area? If you couldn't draw a different triangle, explain why.

B. Draw a triangle with an area of 15 cm². Then, try to draw a different triangle with an area of 15 cm². Do the triangles have the same perimeter? If you couldn't draw a different triangle, explain why.

C. Draw a triangle with sides of length 3 cm, 4 cm, and 5 cm. Then, try to draw a different triangle with these same side lengths. Do the triangles have the same area? If you couldn't draw a different triangle, explain why.

D. A **right triangle** is a triangle that has a right angle. Draw a right triangle with a 30° angle. Then, try to draw a different right triangle with a 30° angle. Do the triangles have the same area? If you couldn't draw a different triangle, explain why.

Assignment Choices

ACE question 7 and unassigned choices from earlier problems

Answers to Problem 6.2

A. See page 68f.

B. Drawings will vary. Common drawings will be of a triangle with base 6 units and height 5 units, a triangle with base 10 units and height 3 units, and a triangle with base 15 units and height 2 units. The perimeters will all be different.

C. One triangle is possible. As students may remember from *Shapes and Designs,* only one triangle is possible from three given side lengths.

D. See page 68g.

Problem 6.2 Follow-Up

1. Summarize what you have discovered from making triangles that fit given constraints. Include your feelings about what kinds of constraints make designing a triangle easy and what kinds of constraints make designing a triangle difficult.

2. Have you discovered any shortcuts for finding areas of triangles? If so, describe them.

6.3 Making Parallelograms from Triangles

In *Shapes and Designs,* you discovered that triangles are useful for building because they are stable figures. If you make a triangle out of three Polystrips, you cannot "squish" it into a different shape. In this problem, you will experiment with paper triangles to try to discover a shortcut for finding the area of a triangle.

Problem 6.3

Draw two triangles on a sheet of grid paper. Make sure the triangles are very different from one another. For each triangle, complete parts A–C.

A. Record the base, height, area, and perimeter of your triangle.

B. Make a copy of your triangle, and cut out both copies. Experiment with putting the two triangles together to make new polygons. Describe and sketch the polygons that are possible.

C. Can you make a parallelogram by piecing together the two identical triangles? If so, record the base, height, area, and perimeter of the parallelogram. How do these measures compare to the measures of the original triangles?

D. Draw a parallelogram on grid paper, and cut it out. Can you cut the parallelogram into two triangles that are the same shape and size? Describe and sketch what you find.

Problem 6.3 Follow-Up

Use what you have learned to find the area and perimeter of this triangle.

At a Glance

***Grouping:
Individuals***

Launch

- Remind students that until now they have found areas of triangles by counting and estimating, and explain that they will now look for shortcuts.

- Review the problem with students, and let them begin work.

Explore

- As you circulate, check that students are making two very different triangles, large enough to work with easily.

Summarize

- Have a few students demonstrate their results.

- Ask questions to focus students on the relationship between the triangles and the parallelogram.

- Discuss the follow-up question.

Answers to Problem 6.2 Follow-Up

1. Answers will vary. Most likely students will find it easiest to construct a triangle when all three dimensions or a base and height measurement are given. Many students probably find it difficult to construct a triangle with a fixed area.

2. See page 68g.

Answers to Problem 6.3

See page 68g.

Answer to Problem 6.3 Follow-Up

area = about 9.6 cm^2, perimeter = 17.6 cm

Assignment Choices

ACE questions 1–6, 8–11, 21, 22, and unassigned choices from previous problems

Answers

Applications

1. area = 28 square units (base = 4, height = 7), perimeter = about 22.6 units (dimensions are 4 by about 7.3)

2. area = 15 square units (base = 5, height = 6), perimeter = about 18.8 units (5 + 6 + about 7.8)

3. area = 6 square units (base = 4, height = 3), perimeter = about 11.3 units (4 + about 3.1 + about 4.2)

4. area = 35 square units (base = 10, height = 7), perimeter = about 27.5 units (10 + about 7.6 + about 9.9)

5. area = 27 square units (base = 9, height = 3), perimeter = about 24.4 units (dimensions are 9 by about 3.2)

6. area = 28 square units (this is a rectangle of area 5 × 4 = 20 square units plus two triangles of combined area 2 × 4 = 8 square units), perimeter = about 23 units (9 + 5 + about 4.5 + about 4.5)

7a. Each triangle has an area of 10 square units.

7b. All the triangles have the same base, height, and area.

7c. Because they all have the same base, height, and area.

As you work on these ACE questions, use your calculator whenever you need it.

Applications

In 1–6, calculate the area and perimeter of the polygon, and briefly explain your reasoning for figures 2, 4, and 6.

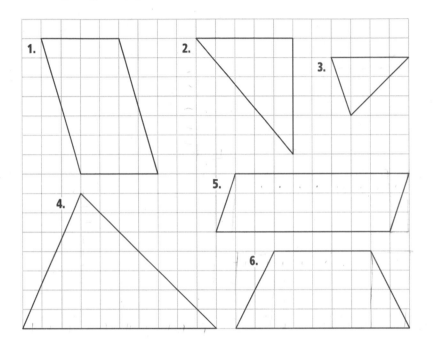

7. On the following page is a *family* of triangles.

    a. Find the area of each triangle.

    b. What patterns do you see?

    c. Why do you think these triangles are called a family?

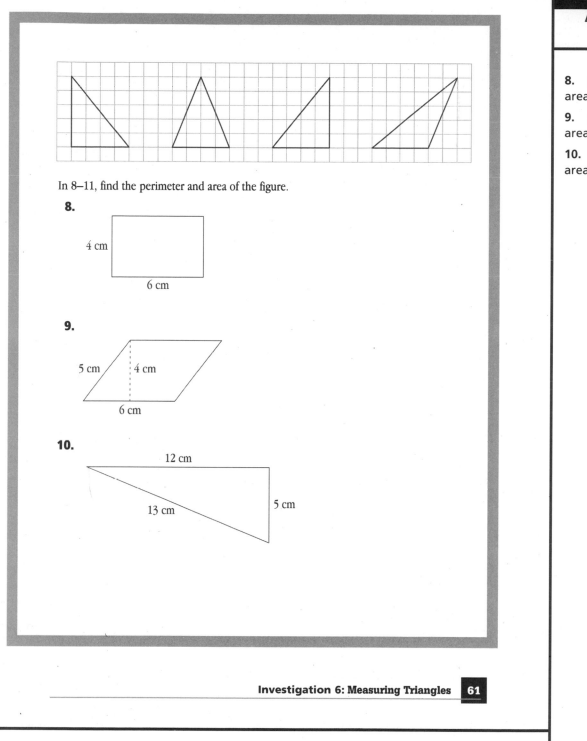

In 8–11, find the perimeter and area of the figure.

8.

4 cm

6 cm

9.

5 cm 4 cm

6 cm

10.

12 cm

13 cm

5 cm

8. perimeter = 20 cm, area = 24 cm²

9. perimeter = 22 cm, area = 24 cm²

10. perimeter = 30 cm, area = 30 cm²

Investigation 6: Measuring Triangles `61`

11. perimeter = 26 cm,
area = 29.75 cm²

12. area = about 6 cm²,
perimeter = about 11 cm

13. area = 6 cm²,
perimeter = 12 cm

11.

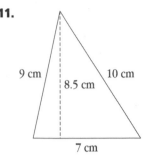

In 12–17, make whatever measurements you need to find the perimeter and area of the figure. Measure in centimeters.

12.

13.

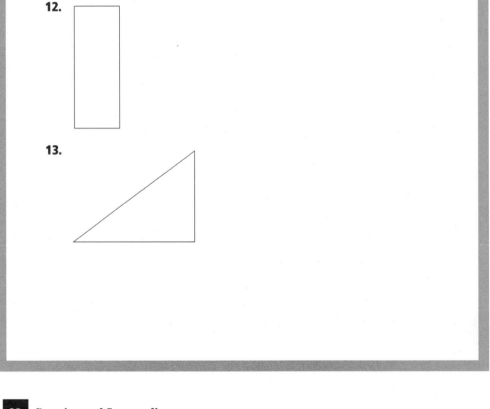

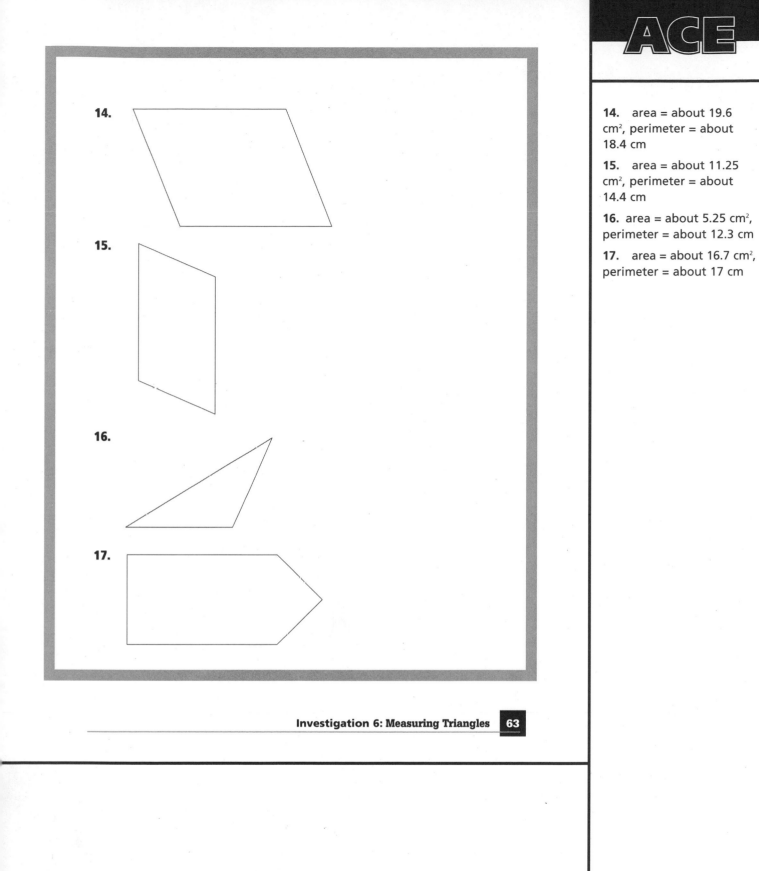

14.

15.

16.

17.

14. area = about 19.6 cm², perimeter = about 18.4 cm

15. area = about 11.25 cm², perimeter = about 14.4 cm

16. area = about 5.25 cm², perimeter = about 12.3 cm

17. area = about 16.7 cm², perimeter = about 17 cm

Investigation 6: Measuring Triangles 63

Connections

18a. Answers will vary. Responses should reflect an appropriate under-standing of selecting one side of the polygon as the base and then measuring the height as the perpen-dicular distance from the highest point of the poly-gon (for the triangle, the vertex opposite the base; for the parallelogram, a point on the side opposite the base) to the base.

18b. Answers will vary. Because the triangle is not resting on an edge, stu-dents may suggest turning the paper 180° and calling the now-bottom side the base. The height would be from the vertex opposite that side straight down to the base.

18c. Answers will vary. Look for evidence that students are seeing the relationships that this investigation is promoting among rectangles, parallel-ograms, and triangles. The product of the base and height gives the area of a parallelogram; with a triangle, we take half of this product.

Connections

18. a. Explain how the base and height could be measured in these figures.

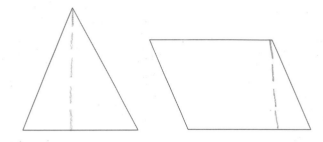

b. Explain how the base and height could be measured in this triangle.

c. Explain how base and height are used to calculate area for parallelograms and triangles. Explain why this method works.

19. A **trapezoid** is a polygon with at least two opposite edges parallel. Below are two trapezoids drawn on grid paper.

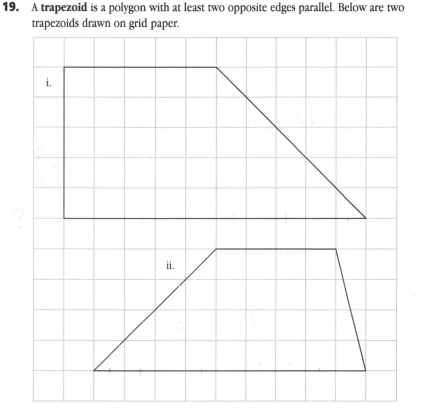

a. Try to find a way to find the area of a trapezoid without having to count each square. Use your method to find the area for each trapezoid. Summarize your method as a rule or a description.

b. How can you find the perimeter of a trapezoid? Use your method to calculate the perimeter of each trapezoid. Summarize your method as a rule or a description.

19a. area of trapezoid i = 37.5 square units; area of trapezoid ii = 26 square units; It is not likely that students will discover the formula for the area of a trapezoid, *area* = $\frac{1}{2} \times (b_1 + b_2) \times h$. They are more likely to discuss dividing a trapezoid into a rectangle and one or two triangles, finding the areas of those figures, and adding the areas.

19b. perimeter of trapezoid i = about 27.2 units; perimeter of trapezoid ii = about 23 units; The perimeter is the sum of the edges of the trapezoid.

20. Possible answer: The hexagon can be subdivided into a rectangle and two triangles. The area of each of the three figures can be found easily and then the results can be added together.

21. area = 42 square inches, perimeter = 26.6 inches

22. area = 72 square inches, perimeter = 35 inches

Extensions

20. Explain how you could calculate the area and perimeter of this hexagon.

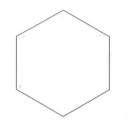

In 21 and 22, find the perimeter and area of the figure.

21.

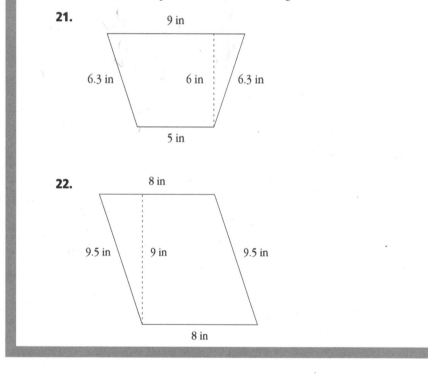

22.

23. You saw earlier that in some parallelograms and triangles, the height falls outside of the shape being measured.

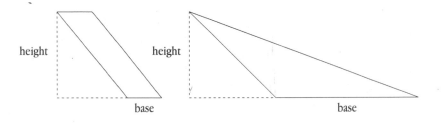

a. The area of the parallelogram can still be calculated by multiplying the base times the height. Write an explanation of why this is true.

b. The area of the triangle can still be calculated by multiplying $\frac{1}{2}$ times the base times the height. Write an explanation of why this is true.

23a. Answers will vary. This is particularly difficult because it is hard to see that the parallelogram can be cut into three pieces and reassembled to form a rectangle with the given base and height as side lengths. Some students may rename the base the height and then describe why the formula works for the new base and height.

23b. Answers will vary. Some students may make two copies of the triangle and show that they can make a parallelogram with the same base and height as the triangle.

Possible Answers

1. Because a triangle is half of a parallelogram, you can find the area of a triangle by measuring its base (any one of its sides) and its height (the perpendicular distance from the vertex opposite the base to the base), multiplying these measures, and taking half the answer. This is like taking half the area of the related parallelogram.

2. To find the perimeter of a triangle, measure all three edges and add the measures together.

3. To find the perimeter of a triangle, a parallelogram, or a rectangle just add the edge lengths. For a triangle, this is $P = a + b + c$, where a, b, and c are the edge lengths. For a parallelogram, this is $P = a + b + c + d$, where a, b, c, and d are the edge lengths. Or, since opposite sides of a parallelogram are equal, you could add the adjacent side lengths, then double that sum. For a rectangle, this is $P = 2 \times (l + w)$, where l is the length and w is the width. For a parallelogram, this is $P = 2 \times (b + s)$, where b is the base and s is the slanted side. Areas of all three polygons can be found by using base (which for rectangles is length) and height (which for rectangles is width). In symbols, the area of a triangle is $A = \frac{1}{2} \times b \times h$. For a rectangle, the area is $A = l \times w$. For parallelograms, the area is $A = b \times h$.

Mathematical Reflections

In this investigation, you invented strategies for finding areas and perimeters of triangles by relating them to parallelograms and rectangles. These questions will help you summarize what you have learned:

1 Describe an efficient way to find the area of a triangle. Be sure to mention the measurements you would need to make and how you would use them to find the area.

2 Describe an efficient way to find the perimeter of a triangle. Be sure to mention the measurements you would need to make and how you would use them to find the perimeter.

3 Summarize what you have discovered about finding areas and perimeters of rectangles, parallelograms, and triangles. Describe the measures you need to make to find the area and perimeter of each figure.

Think about your answers to these questions, discuss your ideas with other students and your teacher, and then write a summary of your findings in your journal.

Are you finalizing your ideas for what you want to put in your park? Have you considered including a picnic area, a tennis court, a basketball court, a water fountain, or rest rooms? What kind of ground covering might you use for the playground area—concrete, sand, grass, wood chips? Keep track of your ideas in your journal.

Tips for the Linguistically Diverse Classroom

Original Rebus The Original Rebus technique is described in detail in *Getting to Know Connected Mathematics*. Students make a copy of the text before it is discussed. During discussion, they generate their own rebuses for words they do not understand as the words are made comprehensible through pictures, objects, or demonstrations. Example: Question 2—key words for which students may make rebuses are *perimeter of a triangle* (bold outline of a triangle), *measurements* (same triangle broken apart so that the sides are not connected), *how would you use them* (same rebus as for measurement but with +, −, ×, ÷ each followed by a question mark).

TEACHING THE INVESTIGATION

6.1 • Finding Measures of Triangles

Like Problem 5.1, this problem asks students to find areas of shapes—eight different triangles—that are not covered with whole squares. The purpose of this activity is to have students *develop and employ reasonable strategies* for finding the areas of these figures (not to use the formula for the area of a triangle): counting, estimating, and talking about ways to deal with parts of grid squares.

Launch

Read the problem, or explain to students that they are again being asked to find perimeters and areas of figures—this time, triangles—that aren't covered with whole squares. Because students have already counted and estimated to find areas of parallelograms and then developed a formula, they might ask you to tell them the formula for triangles. It is not a good idea to tell them the formula. Instead, encourage them to think about what they discovered about finding the areas of parallelograms, and suggest that what they learned may lead them to strategies for finding areas of triangles.

Explore

Have students work in pairs to find the perimeters and areas of the triangles. As you circulate, remind them to record their findings and to explain how they arrived at their answers. Encourage them to look for shortcuts or more efficient ways to use what they already know to find the area of a triangle.

Summarize

Ask students for the measures they found for each figure, and record their answers on the board. Continue to collect answers (even if you have several different measures proposed for the same figure) until all the answers that groups found are recorded.

Figure	Area	Perimeter
A	12 square units	17 units
B	35 square units	29 units
C	12 square units	19.5 units
D	27 square units	24 units
E	16 square units	19.5 units
F	30 square units	26.5 units
G	25.5 square units	24.5 units
H	21 square units	21 units

Focus the class's attention on the chart.

> How did you find these perimeter measurements?

At this point, most students will understand that perimeter is the length around a figure and that they need to measure the three edges of a triangle and add the results. If there are disagreements about the perimeter, you might want to add three more columns to your table, collect the measures of the lengths of the sides, and resolve the perimeter differences. Students will have to estimate to find the lengths of the slanted edges. They can mark the lengths on a strip of paper and then compare the strip to the grid.

How did you find these area measurements?

Students will likely have found area by counting and estimating. Ask whether they tried any other strategies. Again, we are not looking for the formula for the area of a triangle at this point, but the following questions could be used to start students thinking about other strategies:

Which of the triangles are right triangles? *(triangles A, B, and C)* How do you think right triangles are related to rectangles? How could you get a right triangle from a rectangle?

If students have no ideas, demonstrate with two sheets of paper that are the same size. Fold one sheet on the diagonal, and cut along the fold.

What shapes do I have now? *(two right triangles)* How do the two right triangles compare in size and shape? *(Lay one triangle on top of the other to show that they are the same size and shape.)* What measures of the right triangles are the same as measures of the original rectangle?

Hold up the uncut sheet of paper so students can compare the two figures. They should notice that the length and width of the original rectangle are now two edges of the right triangle.

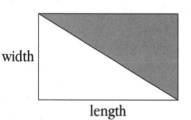

width

length

Are the perimeters of the rectangle and each right triangle the same? *(no)* Why are they different? *(because we have lost two of the edges of the rectangle and gained an edge of a different length)*

Will the areas of the rectangle and the right triangle be the same? *(no)* How do they compare? *(The right triangle is half the original rectangle, so the area of the right triangle is half the area of the rectangle.)*

How might knowing this relationship help you to find the area of any right triangle?

Some students may be able to verbalize that the area of a right triangle is half the area of a rectangle whose length and width are equal to the lengths of the two sides of the triangle that form the right angle. It is not important that all students be able to verbalize this relationship at this time. You just want them to think about how their knowledge of rectangles and parallelograms might help them to find the areas of triangles.

If students seem to be following the conversation, and you want to take it a step further, return to Labsheet 6.1. For triangle A, show how you can make a rectangle with dimensions that are the lengths of the two sides of the triangle that make up the right angle.

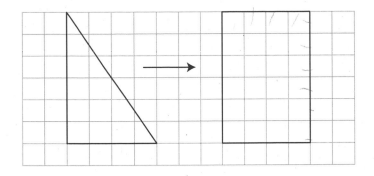

What are the dimensions, perimeter, and area of the rectangle?

Return to the table of triangle measurements, and have students compare the perimeter and area of the rectangle with the triangle. There is no relationship between the perimeters, but students should notice that the area of the rectangle is twice the area of the right triangle. Have students test whether this pattern holds for the other two right triangles (B and C).

After this further investigation of right triangles and rectangles, you might again ask students how knowing the relationship between rectangles and right triangles can help them to find the area of right triangles. Because the other triangles are not right triangles, you will probably want to leave them until after the class investigates the relationship between parallelograms and triangles in Problem 6.3.

6.2 • Designing Triangles Under Constraints

In this activity, which is similar to Problem 5.2, students are asked to construct several triangles with given dimensions, areas, or angles. In each case, they are asked whether they can draw a different triangle for the same constraints and whether the areas or perimeters of the two triangles differ.

Launch

Discuss the overview of base and height on page 58 of the student edition. The *height* of a triangle is the perpendicular distance from one vertex to the opposite side. In the first triangle shown, the height falls inside the figure. In the right triangle, the height is one of the sides. For the third triangle, the height falls outside the figure.

You may want to use the triangles from Problem 6.1 to help students understand height. Ask what the height of triangle A is. If someone tells you 6 units (which is correct), ask him or her to explain why. If no one figures this out, tell students the answer, and explain that it is the distance from the side you have identified as the base to the vertex opposite the base. Check for understanding by having students find the heights of triangles B–H.

Explore

Each student should make his or her own drawings. Pairs can discuss how to approach each part, then check each other's drawings.

As you circulate, remind students to label their drawings so that they are easy to refer to during the summary. Pairs that finish early can work on the follow-up questions.

Summarize

Start the summary by discussing the first follow-up question, which asks students what they have found from making these designs.

> What kinds of constraints make drawing a triangle easy? What kinds of constraints make drawing a triangle difficult?

If a student identifies a certain type of information as difficult, ask the other students whether they came up with strategies for drawing triangles under that kind of constraint.

> Were there any questions for which you could make only one triangle to fit the constraints?

If students say no, ask them to share what they found for part C. If they give two different triangles, the second is probably a different orientation of the first. This idea was discussed in the *Shapes and Designs* unit.

Have students share their responses to the parts of the problem. After one student gives an answer, ask if anyone has a different answer. You want students to notice that fixing the base and height of a triangle does not limit the shape of the triangle but does fix the area.

Students may see that right triangles are half of a rectangle, but most will not yet have developed strategies for finding areas of triangles that are not right triangles.

6.3 • Making Parallelograms from Triangles

This problem is designed to help students see that a triangle is half of a parallelogram. Students design two triangles, make two copies of each, and experiment with the two pairs of triangles to find all the ways they can arrange them to make a new polygon.

You want students to realize that two congruent triangles can always be arranged to make a parallelogram. This relationship between triangles and parallelograms, and the relationship between parallelograms and rectangles, means that we can always make a parallelogram from two identical triangles and then make that parallelogram into a rectangle. This problem lays the conceptual foundation for students to invent or rediscover the formula for finding the area of a triangle, *area* $= \frac{1}{2} \times base \times height$, or $A = \frac{1}{2} \times b \times h$.

Launch

Remind students that they have, until now, found areas of triangles by counting and estimating. In this activity, they will look for relationships that might help them develop an easier way to find areas of triangles.

Read the problem with your students. When you feel they understand what to do, let them begin work on the problem. (If you do not have an overhead projector for students to demonstrate how they put their triangles together to form parallelograms, have them work on inch grid paper and tape their triangles to construction paper.)

Explore

Students should make and cut their own figures but can work in pairs to share results. As you visit the students, verify that they are making two very different triangles and that the triangles are large enough to work with easily. Some students may only find a couple of polygons and then stop. Ask these students some questions:

> What happens if you flip one of the triangles over? Can you create a different polygon?

> Can the triangles be matched on a different side? Does this create a different polygon?

Make sure students explain how they created their parallelograms (some of which may be rectangles). Some may see this more easily by labeling the vertices of the triangles.

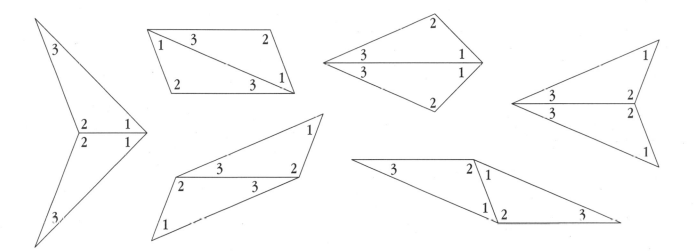

When students complete the problem, ask them to work on the follow-up questions.

Summarize

Have two or three students demonstrate, perhaps at the overhead projector, all the different polygons they made from a pair of congruent triangles.

Ask questions to focus students on the relationship of the triangles to the parallelogram.

> Were you always able to make a parallelogram from two identical triangles? (*yes*)

> What do two identical triangles and the parallelogram made from them have in common? (*The edge lengths of the parallelogram are two of the three edge lengths of the triangle.*)

> From your experimentation and what you already know about finding areas of parallelograms and rectangles, how can you find the area of a triangle without counting and estimating?

A triangle is half of a parallelogram, so the area of a triangle is half of the area of the corresponding parallelogram. The area of the parallelogram can be found by multiplying its base times its height. The area of the triangle is half of this product. Since the base and height of the triangle are the same as the base and height of the corresponding parallelogram, the area of a triangle is half the product of its base times its height. If the formula for the area of a triangle ($A = \frac{1}{2} \times b \times b$) is given, have students return to the triangles in Problem 6.1 and test it. If no one can give the formula, say that you notice an interesting pattern, and describe the pattern. Ask your students whether they think it makes sense and will always work.

Conclude the summary by discussing how to find the perimeter and area of the triangle in the follow-up.

What measurements do you need to find the perimeter of the given triangle? (*all three edge lengths*) What are the edge lengths of this triangle? (*about 8 cm, 3.3 cm, and 6.3 cm*) What is the perimeter of this triangle? (*about 17.6 cm*)

What measurements do you need to find the area of the given triangle? (*base and height*) What are the base and the height of this triangle? (*base = about 8 cm, height = about 2.4 cm*) How can you use these measurements to find the area of the triangle? (*Multiply the base times the height and take half of the product; area = about 9.6 cm².*)

How could we test to see whether the answer is reasonable? (*Cover the triangle with a transparent centimeter grid, and count and estimate the number of squares inside the triangle.*)

Additional Answers

Answers to Problem 6.2

A.   Drawings will vary. You can draw many triangles—actually, an infinite number—with the same base and height. If students have trouble seeing this, ask them to imagine sliding a line (representing the triangle's height) from one end of the base to the other. The areas of the triangles will be the same, but the perimeters will be different. Possible drawings:

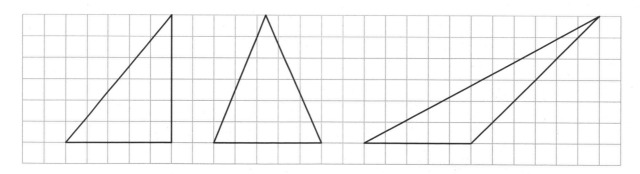

D. Drawings will vary. You can draw an infinite number of right triangles with a 30° angle. The triangles will have different areas and different perimeters, but they will all have the same angle measures and the same shape. Possible drawings:

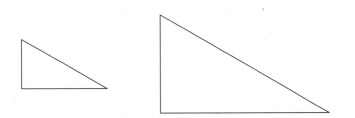

For the Teacher: Triangle Similarity

Triangles with the same angle measures are said to be similar. Similarity is not an idea with which most of your students will be familiar, and it is not suggested that you discuss it at this time. The ideas of similarity are covered in the *Stretching and Shrinking* unit.

Answers to Problem 6.2 Follow-Up

2. Answers will vary. Few, if any, students will have discovered the formula for area of a triangle, *area* $= \frac{1}{2} \times base \times height$. If someone knows the formula, it is likely an adult or older sibling gave it to the student. If a student presents the formula to the class, ask the student to explain why it makes sense and why it works. If the student can't explain, ask the class to think about what the formula is measuring and whether it makes sense.

Answers to Problem 6.3

A. Answers will vary.

B. Answers will vary. Students should be able to make six polygons from a pair of congruent triangles (if the triangles have three different edge lengths).

C. Answers will vary. Students should be able to make three parallelograms from a pair of congruent triangles (if the triangles have three different edge lengths).

D. Any parallelogram can be cut into two congruent triangles by cutting along either diagonal.

Going Around in Circles

In this investigation, students discover how the diameter of a circle is related to its circumference and area. The problems in this investigation lay the foundation for students to develop an understanding of the number π (pi), which represents the number of diameters needed to surround a circle (and the number of "radius squares" needed to cover a circle). Some students will have already seen the expressions $C = \pi d$ and $A = \pi r^2$. This investigation gives meaning to these symbols.

In Problem 7.1, Pricing Pizza, students find the radii, areas, and circumferences of three different sizes of pizza and use this information to evaluate the pricing scheme for the pizzas. In Problem 7.2, Surrounding a Circle, students measure the diameters and circumferences of several circular objects. By organizing their data into a table and making a coordinate graph, they discover that it takes slightly more than three diameters to equal the circumference of a circle. Problem 7.3, Covering a Circle, asks students to find ways to estimate the area of a given circle. In Problem 7.4, "Squaring" a Circle, students cover circles with "radius squares"—squares with edge lengths equal to the circle's radius—and discover that a little more than three radius squares are needed to equal the area of any circle. In Problem 7.5, Replacing Trees, students use their new knowledge of circumference and area to investigate a real-world problem.

Mathematical and Problem-Solving Goals

- **To develop techniques for estimating the area of a circle**

- **To discover that it takes slightly more than three diameters to equal the circumference of a circle**

- **To discover that it takes slightly more than three radius squares to equal the area of the circle**

- **To use ideas about area and perimeter to solve practical problems**

Materials		
Problem	**For students**	**For the teacher**
All	Calculators, compass (1 per student), centimeter grid paper (provided as a blackline master)	Transparencies 7.1 to 7.5 (optional)
7.1	String, scissors	9-cm, 12-cm, and 15-cm circles cut from transparent grid paper (optional)
7.2	Several circular objects, tape measures	
7.4	Labsheet 7.4 (1 per student), scissors	

Student Pages 69–81   Teaching the Investigation 81a–81j

Going Around in Circles

You encounter circles every day of your life. They are one of the most useful shapes. Circles are used for making things like tools, toys, and transportation vehicles, and everyday items like bottle caps, compact discs, and coins. Take a minute to think of how different your life would be without circles.

There are at least four measurements that are useful for describing the size of a **circle**: *diameter, radius, area,* and *circumference.* The **diameter** of a circle is any line segment that extends from a point on the circle, through the center, to another point on the circle. The **radius** is any line segment from the center to a point on the circle. **Circumference** means *perimeter* in the language of circles—it is the distance around the circle.

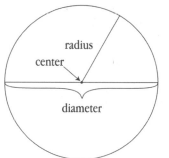

7.1

Pricing Pizza

Launch

- Review the introduction to the investigation and make sure students understand the meaning of *circumference*, *radius*, and *diameter*.

- Read Problem 7.1.

- Talk about how to construct models of pizzas.

Explore

- Have students work in pairs to measure the circles.

- Ask students to write the report suggested in the follow-up.

Summarize

- As a class, record students' circle measurements and discuss strategies.

- Discuss the reports students wrote for the follow-up.

Assignment Choices

ACE question 14 and unassigned choices from earlier problems. Ask students to bring in circular objects for use in the next problem.

It is easy to measure the diameter and radius of a circle, but measuring the area and circumference is not as easy. You can't cover the circle with an exact number of square tiles to compute the area, and you can't easily use a ruler to measure its circumference.

As you work on the problems in this investigation, look for connections between a circle's diameter, radius, area, and circumference. Search for clues that tell when each of these measurements gives useful information about a circular object in a given situation.

7.1 Pricing Pizza

Many pizza restaurants sell small, medium, and large pizzas— usually measured by the diameter of a circular pie. Of course, the prices are different for the three sizes. Do you think a large pizza is usually the best buy?

Problem 7.1

The Sole D'Italia Pizzeria sells small, medium, and large pizzas. A small is 9 inches in diameter, a medium is 12 inches in diameter, and a large is 15 inches in diameter. Prices for cheese pizzas are $6.00 for small, $9.00 for medium, and $12.00 for large.

A. Draw a 9-inch, a 12-inch, and a 15-inch "pizza" on centimeter grid paper. Let 1 centimeter of the grid paper represent 1 inch on the pizza. Estimate the radius, circumference, and area of each pizza. (You may want to use string to help you find the circumference.)

B. Which measurement—radius, diameter, circumference, or area—seems most closely related to price? Explain your answer.

■ Problem 7.1 Follow-Up

Use your results to write a report about what you consider to be the best value of the pizza options at Sole D'Italia.

Answers to Problem 7.1

A. Students' measurements should be close to those in this table.

Size	Diameter	Radius	Circumference	Area
small	9 inches	4.5 inches	28.3 inches	63.6 square inches
medium	12 inches	6 inches	37.7 inches	113.1 square inches
large	15 inches	7.5 inches	47.1 inches	176.7 square inches

B. Answers will vary. Most students will say that the diameter is most closely related to the price because, as the diameter changes by 3 inches, the price changes by $3.

Answer to Problem 7.1 Follow-Up

See page 81h.

7.2 ## Surrounding a Circle

Mathematicians have found a relationship between the diameter and circumference of a circle. You can try to discover this relationship by measuring many different circles and looking for patterns. The patterns you discover can help you develop a shortcut for finding the circumference of a circle.

At a Glance

Grouping:
Pairs

> ### Problem 7.2
>
> In this problem, you will work with a collection of circular objects.
>
> **A.** Use a tape measure to find the diameter and circumference of each object. Record your results in a table with these column headings:
>
> | Object | Diameter | Circumference |
>
> **B.** Make a coordinate graph of your data. Use the horizontal axis for diameter and the vertical axis for circumference.
>
> **C.** Study your table and your graph, looking for patterns and relationships that will allow you to predict the circumference from the diameter. Test your ideas on some other circular objects. Once you think you have found a pattern, answer this question: What do you think the relationship is between the diameter and the circumference of a circle?

■ Problem 7.2 Follow-Up

1. How can you find the circumference of a circle if you know its diameter?

2. How can you find the diameter of the circle if you know its circumference?

3. Use the relationships you discovered in the problem to calculate the circumferences of the pizzas from Problem 7.1. How do your calculations compare to your estimates?

Launch

■ Read the problem with the class, emphasizing that they will be looking for a shortcut for finding the circumference of a circle.

■ Supply groups with circular objects, or have them use objects they have brought from home.

Explore

■ Have students work in pairs to measure the circular objects.

■ Do part B of the problem as a class. (*optional*)

Summarize

■ As a class, look for patterns in the data.

■ Discuss the relationship between diameter and circumference, and introduce the number pi.

Answers to Problem 7.2

A. Answers will vary. The circumference for each object should be a little more than 3 times the diameter.

B. Graphs will vary. Points should fall in approximately a straight line.

C. The circumference is a little more than 3 times the diameter.

Answers to Problem 7.2 Follow-Up

1. Possible answer: Add together 3 diameters and a bit more, or multiply the diameter by 3 and add a bit more.

2. Possible answer: Divide the circumference by 3 and subtract a bit from the result.

3. See page 81h.

Assignment Choices

ACE questions 1–5 (have students find the circumference at this time and the area later), 6–8, and unassigned choices from earlier problems

only circumference

7.3

Covering a Circle

At a Glance

Grouping:
Pairs

Launch

- As a class, review methods for finding perimeters and areas of shapes students have studied so far.

- Explain that students will try to find a method for finding the area of a circle.

Explore

- Have students work in pairs to find the area of the circle and to explore different strategies.

- Help students that are struggling, by asking questions that will help them cut down on the work by using symmetry.

Summarize

- Have students share their answers and strategies.

Assignment Choices

Unassigned choices from earlier problems

In the last problem, you discovered a pattern for finding the circumference of a circle. Do you think there is a similar pattern for finding the area of a circle?

> **Problem 7.3**
>
> Find as many different ways as you can to estimate the area of the circle below. For each method, give your area estimate and carefully describe how you found it. Include drawings in your descriptions if they help show what you did.

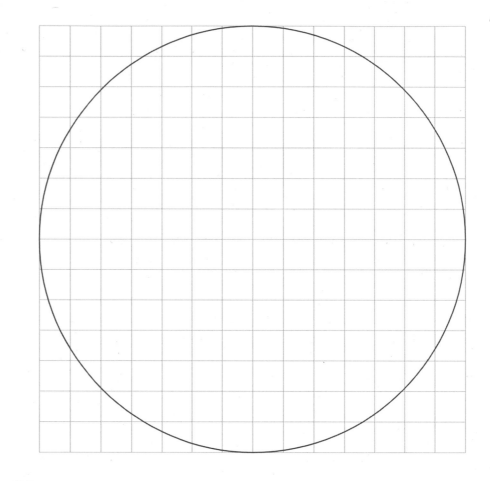

Answers to Problem 7.3

Strategies will vary. The area of the circle is 153.86 square units when 3.14 is used for π. A reasonable answer for students who use some means of covering and counting is between 150 and 160 square units.

■ **Problem 7.3 Follow-Up**

Will a circle with a diameter equal to half the diameter of the circle in the problem have an area equal to half the area of that circle? Why or why not?

7.4 "Squaring" a Circle

In Investigations 5 and 6, you learned some things about parallelograms and triangles by comparing them to rectangles. Now you will find out more about circles by comparing them to squares.

Labsheet 7.4 shows the three circles that are drawn below. A portion of each circle is covered by a shaded square. The sides of each shaded square are the same length as the radius of the circle. We call such a square a "radius square."

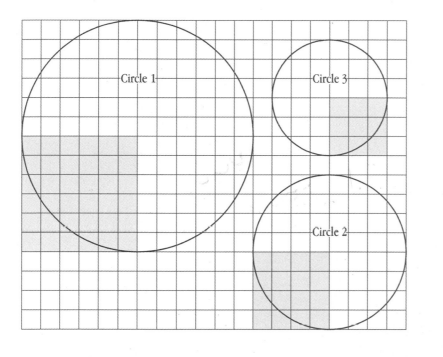

Circle 1

Circle 3

Circle 2

Launch

■ Read the problem to the class.

■ Demonstrate how to cover a circle with radius squares. (*optional*)

Explore

■ Have students work individually to cover the circles with radius squares, then share their results with a partner.

■ As you circulate, make sure students are recording results in a table.

Summarize

■ Have students share their strategies for covering the circles.

■ Ask questions to help them see the connection between their work with circles and the number pi.

Answers to Problem 7.3 Follow-Up

No, the area of the small circle would be less than half the area of the large circle. The two small circles in the illustration each have a diameter equal to half the diameter of the large circle. The combined area of these circles is much less than the area of the large circle.

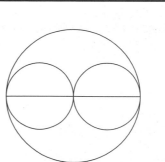

Assignment Choices

ACE questions 1–13 and unassigned choices from earlier problems

+ #15

Problem 7.4

A. For each circle, cut out several copies of the radius square from a sheet of centimeter grid paper. Find out how many radius squares it takes to cover the circle. You may cut the radius squares into parts if you need to. Record your data in a table with these column headings:

Circle	Radius of circle	Area of radius square	Area of circle	Number of radius squares needed

B. Now draw a couple of your own circles on grid paper. You can use circles from the objects you measured in Problem 7.2 and from your Shapes Set. Make radius squares for each circle, and find out how many radius squares it takes to cover each circle. Add this data to your table.

C. Describe any patterns you see in your data.

D. If you were asked to estimate the area of any circle in "radius squares," what would you report as the best estimate?

■ **Problem 7.4 Follow-Up**

1. How can you find the area of a circle if you know the diameter or the radius?

2. How can you find the diameter or radius of a circle if you know the area?

Did you know?

You have discovered that the area of a circle is a *little more than 3* times the radius squared. You have also found that the distance around a circle is a *little more than 3* times the diameter. There is a special name given to this number that is a little more than 3.

In 1706, William Jones used π (pronounced "pi"), the Greek letter for *p*, to represent this number. He used the symbol to stand for the *periphery,* or distance around, a circle with a diameter of 1 unit.

As early as 2000 B.C., the Babylonians *knew* that π was more than 3! Their estimate for π was $3\frac{1}{8}$. By the fifth century, Chinese mathematician Tsu Chung-Chi wrote that π was somewhere between 3.1415926 and 3.1415927. From 1436 until 1874, the known value of π went from 14 places past the decimal to 707 places. Computers have been used to calculate millions more digits, and today we know that the digits will never repeat and will never end. This kind of number is called *irrational.*

Answers to Problem 7.4

A. See page 81i.

B. Answers will vary.

C. Answers will vary. Ideally, students will notice that it takes a little more than three radius squares to cover any circle.

D. Possible answer: The area of any circle is a little bit more than three radius squares.

Answers to Problem 7.4 Follow-Up

See page 81i.

7.5 Replacing Trees

In large cities filled with streets and concrete buildings, trees are a valuable part of the environment. In New York City, people who damage or destroy a tree are required by law to plant new trees as community service. Two replacement rules have been used:

Diameter rule: The total *diameter* of the new tree(s) must equal the diameter of the tree(s) that were damaged or destroyed.

Area rule: The total *area of the cross section* of the new tree(s) must equal the area of the cross section of the tree(s) that were damaged or destroyed.

Problem 7.5

The following diagram shows the cross section of a damaged tree and the cross section of the new trees that will be planted to replace it.

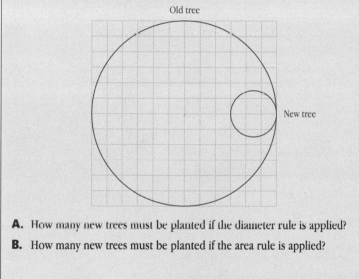

Old tree

New tree

A. How many new trees must be planted if the diameter rule is applied?

B. How many new trees must be planted if the area rule is applied?

■ Problem 7.5 Follow-Up

Which rule do you think is fairer? Use mathematics to explain your answer.

7.5

Replacing Trees

At a Glance

Grouping: Small Groups

Launch

- Read the problem with the class, making sure they understand the replacement rules.

Explore

- Have groups of three or four work on the problem and follow-up.

- As you circulate, make sure groups are providing explanations and mathematical reasons for their choice.

Summarize

- Have students share their answers and strategies for the problem and follow-up.

Answers to Problem 7.5

A. Using the diameter rule, only four new trees would be needed to replace the old tree because the diameter of the old tree is four times the diameter of each new tree. Students can verify this by observing that the diameter of the new tree is 3 units and the diameter of the old tree is 12 units.

B. Using the area rule, about $\frac{113}{7} = 16$ trees would be needed to replace the old tree. The small circle has a radius of 1.5 units, so its area is about 7 square units. The large tree has a radius of 6 units, so its area is about 113 square units.

Answer to Problem 7.5 Follow-up

Answers will vary. See the "Summarize" section on page 81h.

Assignment Choices

ACE questions 16, 17, and unassigned choices from earlier problems

Assessment

It is appropriate to use Check-Up 2 and Quiz B after this problem. Centimeter rulers are required for Check-Up 2.

Answers

Applications

1. circumference = about 28.3 inches, area = about 63.6 square inches

2. radius = 13 inches, circumference = about 81.6 inches, area = about 530.7 square inches

3. circumference = about 7.1 inches

4. diameter = 80 feet, circumference = about 251.2 feet, area = about 5024 square feet

5. album: radius = 6 inches, circumference = about 37.7 inches, area = about 113 square inches; compact disc: radius = 2.5 inches, circumference = about 15.7 inches, area = about 19.6 square inches

6. area = about 9.6 cm², perimeter = about 11 cm

7. area = about 4.3 cm², perimeter = about 9.6 cm

As you work on these ACE questions, use your calculator whenever you need it.

Applications

In 1–5, use the given measurements of a circle to find the other measurements. You may want to make scale drawings on grid paper to help find the missing measurements.

1. A dinner plate has a diameter of about 9 inches. Find its circumference and area.

2. A bicycle wheel is about 26 inches in diameter. Find its radius, circumference, and area.

3. A soft-drink can is about 2.25 inches in diameter. What is its circumference?

4. If the spray from a lawn sprinkler makes a circle 40 feet in radius, what are the approximate diameter, circumference, and area of the circle of lawn watered?

5. A standard long-playing record album has a 12-inch diameter; a compact disc has a 5-inch diameter. Find the radius, circumference, and area of each.

In 6–8, estimate, as accurately as possible, the area and perimeter of the figure. Make your measurements in centimeters.

6.

7.

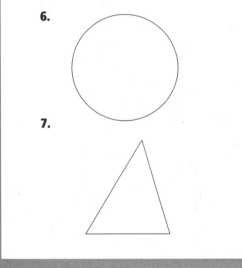

8.

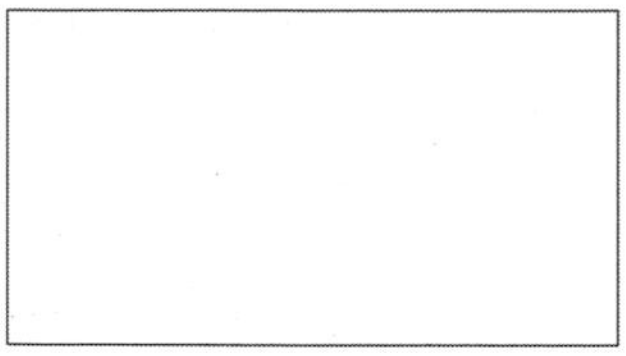

Connections

Some everyday circular objects are commonly described by giving their radius or diameter. In 9–12, explain what useful information (if any) you would get from calculating the area or circumference of the circle.

9. a 3.5-inch-diameter computer disk

10. a 21-inch-diameter bicycle wheel

11. a 12-inch-diameter water pipe

12. a lawn sprinkler that sprays a 15-meter-radius section of lawn

---

Did you know?

3.14159265358979323846264338327950288419716939937510 . . . How many places can you remember? One man was known to have memorized π to 50,000 places! How important is it to be exact about this number? Actually, precision engines can be built using an approximation of 3.1416. You can calculate the earth's circumference within a fraction of an inch by knowing π out to only 10 places. So unless you love to memorize, 3.14 or the fraction $\frac{22}{7}$ are close enough approximations to make pretty good measurements.

---

8. area = 14 cm², perimeter = 15.6 cm

Connections

9. Possible answer: The area of a computer disk tells you something about the storage space on the disk.

10. Possible answer: The circumference of a bicycle wheel tells you how far the bike travels in one revolution.

11. Possible answer: The diameter (and related cross-sectional area) of a pipe will tell how much water can flow through the pipe.

12. Possible answer: The area of a lawn sprinkler's spray would let you estimate how much of your lawn will get watered at each location the device is used and thus will allow you to estimate how long it will take to water your lawn.

13a. radius = about 4 inches, circumference = about 25 inches, area = about 50 square inches.

13b. The circumference will be about half—about 12.5 inches The area, however, will be only one fourth as much—about 12.5 square inches

14a. 6 × 8.5 = 51 square feet

14b. 2 × 6 + 2 × 8.5 = 29 feet

14c. The perimeter is 29 feet, and the walls are 6 feet high, so there is 6 × 29 = 174 square feet of wall space (minus any windows or doors). They will need $\frac{174}{50}$ pints. (Because this is about $3\frac{1}{2}$ pints, they will need to buy 4 pints.)

14d. Answers will vary.

15. Pizza sizes are usually given by diameter. The area is a logical measure of the amount of pizza. However, the radius and circumference are also defensible answers, because, as any of the four measures of a circle increase or decrease, so do the other three. Therefore, since all four measures are related, any of them are technically plausible as indicators of the size of the pizza.

16a. The polygon has 360 sides.

16b. The perimeter is 360 turtle steps, since there are 360 sides and each side is 1 turtle step long.

16c. See page 81i.

13. A large burner on a standard electric stove is about 8 inches in diameter.

 a. What are the radius, area, and circumference of the burner?

 b. How would the area and circumference of a smaller 4-inch-diameter burner compare to the area and circumference of the 8-inch burner? Check your answers with calculations.

14. Karl and Aimeé are building a playhouse for their little sister. The floor of the playhouse will be a rectangle that is 6 feet by $8\frac{1}{2}$ feet.

 a. How much carpeting will Karl and Aimeé need to cover the floor?

 b. How much molding will they need around the edges of the floor to hold the carpet in place?

 c. The walls will be 6 feet high. A pint of paint covers about 50 square feet. How much paint will they need to paint the inside walls? Explain your answer.

 d. Make your own plan for a playhouse. Figure out how much carpeting, wood, paint, and molding you would need to build the playhouse.

15. Which measurement of a circular pizza—diameter, radius, circumference, or area—best indicates its size?

16. The Logo instructions on the following page draw a polygon with so many sides that it looks like a circle.

 a. How many sides does this polygon have?

 b. What is the perimeter of the polygon, in turtle steps?

 c. *Approximately* how many turtle steps would it take for the turtle to walk the path from point A to point B? Explain your answer.

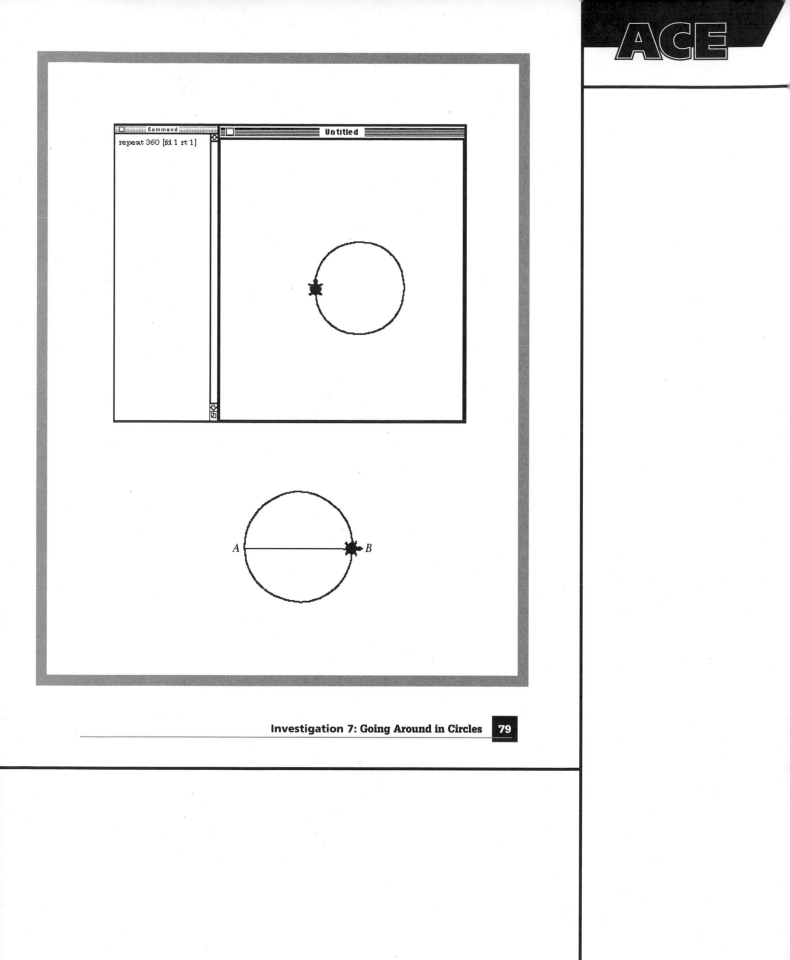

Extensions

17a. Since the string is 60 cm long, each edge of the equilateral triangle will be $\frac{60}{3}$, or 20, cm long. The triangle, drawn on a grid, has a height of about 17.3 cm. The area would be $\frac{1}{2} \times b \times h$, or $0.5 \times 20 \times 17.3 = 173$ cm². The square would have edges of $\frac{60}{4}$, or 15, cm, so its area would be 15×15, or 225, cm². The hexagon would have edges of $\frac{60}{6}$, or 10, cm. To find the area, you can subdivide the hexagon into a rectangle and two triangles.

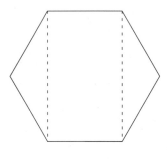

The rectangle has an area of 10×17, or 170, cm². The triangles each have a height of about 5 cm and a base of about 17 cm, so the area of each one is $0.5 \times 5 \times 17$, or 42.5 cm². Adding the areas of the rectangles and the two triangles, gives a total area of 255 cm². A honeycomb might be covered with hexagons because, of all the regular polygons that tile a surface, the hexagon has the greatest area. Therefore, cells with hexagonal cross sections allow the most room for storing honey.

17b.–f. See page 81i.

Extensions

17. Suppose you tie together the ends of a piece of string to form a loop that is 60 centimeters long.

   a. Suppose you arranged the string to form an equilateral triangle. What would the area of the enclosed space be? What would the area be if you formed square? A regular hexagon?

   Think back to the work you did in *Shapes and Designs*. Why do you think the surface of a honeycomb is covered with hexagons?

   b. Of all the rectangles with a perimeter of 60 centimeters, which has greatest area?

   c. Of all the triangles with a perimeter of 60 centimeters, which has greatest area?

   d. How does the area of a regular octagon with a perimeter of 60 centimeters compare to the areas of a triangle, a square, and a hexagon with perimeters of 60 centimeters?

   e. What happens to the enclosed area as the 60-centimeter perimeter is used to make regular polygons of more and more sides? (If you have access to a computer and the Logo programming language, you might use the computer to draw these figures.)

   f. As the number of sides of a polygon gets larger and larger, what shape does the polygon eventually resemble?

Mathematical Reflections

In this investigation, you discovered strategies for finding the area and circumference (perimeter) of a circle. You examined relationships between the circumference and the diameter of a circle and between the area and the radius of a circle. These questions will help you summarize what you have learned:

1 Describe how you can find the circumference of a circle by measuring the radius or the diameter. If you need to, explain your thinking by using a specific circle.

2 Describe how you can find the area of a circle by measuring its radius or its diameter. If you need to, explain your thinking by using a specific circle. Why is your method useful?

Think about your answers to these questions, discuss your ideas with other students and your teacher, and then write a summary of your findings in your journal.

You will soon be designing your layout for the city park. How might your new information about circles help you? What objects in your park might be in the shape of a circle—a flower garden, a water fountain?

Tips for the Linguistically Diverse Classroom

Original Rebus The Original Rebus technique is described in detail in *Getting to Know Connected Mathematics*. Students make a copy of the text before it is discussed. During discussion, they generate their own rebuses for words they do not understand as the words are made comprehensible through pictures, objects, or demonstrations. Example: Question 1—key words for which students may make rebuses are *circle* (the bold outline of a circle), *radius* (a circle with the radius drawn with a bold line), *diameter* (a circle with the diameter drawn with a bold line).

TEACHING THE INVESTIGATION

This problem asks students to think about how a pizza is priced relative to its diameter, radius, circumference, and area. Students are asked to find these measures for three different circular pizzas and to decide which measures are most closely related to price. The purpose of the problem is to encourage students to think about measuring circles, not to introduce formulas. We envision them using counting and estimating strategies to find area and circumference. Problems 7.2–7.4 will help them discover the formulas for the circumference and area of a circle.

Launch

Discuss the ideas presented in the overview of the investigation in the student edition. Make sure students understand what the diameter, radius, and circumference of a circle are.

Read Problem 7.1 with the class. It would be helpful to have models of the three pizzas (cut from transparent grid paper) as you review the questions posed in the problem. Discuss how students can use a compass to make their own models by drawing circles on centimeter grid paper using a 1 inch = 1 centimeter scale. If they have trouble with this scaled model, let them use large sheets of inch grid paper or tape together several sheets to make circles the actual size of the pizzas.

Students are asked to find several pieces of data to help them answer the questions. Remind them to organize the information they collect so they can look for patterns and make comparisons more easily.

Explore

Have students work in pairs or small groups to find the radius, circumference, and area of each circle. As you visit the groups, make sure they are recording their findings and can explain how they arrived at their answers. After students have completed the problem, have them write the report suggested in the follow-up.

Summarize

On the board or overhead projector, record the measurements that students found for the radius, circumference, and area of each circle. Discuss how they found the measurements and whether any seem unreasonable. Because students are counting and estimating, circumferences and areas will vary but should be within a reasonable range.

Size	Diameter	Radius	Circumference	Area
small	9 inches	4.5 inches	28.3 inches	63.6 square inches
medium	12 inches	6 inches	37.7 inches	113.1 square inches
large	15 inches	7.5 inches	47.1 inches	176.7 square inches

Since students have found formulas for perimeter and area of several polygons, they may ask what the formulas are for circumference and area of a circle. They may tire of fitting a string and counting squares after just a few examples. Reflect the question back to them.

Do you see any patterns in the measurements that might help you predict circumference and area?

Do not give the formulas now unless students see the relationships among diameter, radius, circumference, and area and can explain why they make sense.

Discuss the answers to part B, and have students present the reports they wrote for the follow-up. Students will probably need help in deciding how to compare the pizzas. Many will say that the diameter is most closely related to price because as it changes by 3 inches, the price changes by $3.00.

7.2 • Surrounding a Circle

In this problem, students measure the diameters and circumferences of several circles, organize their data in a table, and look for patterns. The goal is for them to find a pattern, rule, or formula for finding the circumference of a circle. After working on Problem 7.1, students are probably anxious to find an easier way to compute the circumference of a circle.

Launch

Read the problem with the class. Emphasize that they are looking for patterns that may help them discover a shortcut for finding the circumference of a circle.

Supply students with several circular objects—such as soda cans, records, wastebaskets, coins, and compact discs—or have them use objects they have brought from home. You might want to have set(s) of objects for pairs of students to measure and share with other groups. Set aside a few extra circular objects for groups to test their ideas for finding circumference.

Explore

Students can work in pairs to make the measurements but should record the data individually.

You could save some time by doing part B (making a coordinate graph) as a class; write the column heads and draw the coordinate axes on the board prior to the start of the activity. Have each group record the measures for one circular object in the table and plot the data point on the graph; you can easily refer to both organization schemes during the summary. Plotting points should be a review exercise for students (coordinate graphs were studied in the *Data About Us* unit).

Summarize

Ask students to look at the information in both the graph and the table and to see whether they disagree with any entries. Discuss and resolve any disagreements.

> Mathematicians have found a relationship between diameter and circumference. By looking at our data, can you guess what that relationship is?

The graph should be very close to a straight line, which indicates that the relationship between circumference and diameter is linear. For each unit of diameter, the circumference increases by the same amount—a little more than 3 units. This can also be seen in the table by comparing the diameter and circumference measures.

Students may observe that the circumference is bigger than the diameter but go no further. When asked how much bigger, they may talk about the difference between the two amounts. If so, ask them to estimate the circumferences of circles with diameters that are not displayed on the graph or table—perhaps for a circle much larger than those previously measured.

What you want students to notice is that the relationship is multiplicative and that the circumference is always the diameter times a little bit more than 3.

After students have verbalized the relationship between diameter and circumference, have them test the idea on a few new objects. Measure the diameter of an object, have the class predict its circumference, then check their prediction by measuring. After a few examples, push for a more exact number than "a little bit more than 3." You might find the ratio of the circumference to the diameter for all the circular objects measured (which should be close to 3.1 or 3.2) and then introduce the number π (pi). (For our purposes, 3.14 is close enough, although you will want to tell students that this is a rounded number. For the curious student, the value of π to nine decimal places is 3.141592654.)

After students have used π to find the circumferences of a few circles, have them test circles they have already found circumferences for—such as the pizzas in Problem 7.1—to see how close the measurements are. Then, have them work backward to find the diameter of a circle when the circumference is given.

7.3 • Covering a Circle

This problem asks students to find the area of a given circle. The purpose is not for them to find or use a formula but to see the need for a shortcut—a formula—for finding the area of a circle. Problem 7.4 will introduce a method for finding the area of a circle.

Launch

A review of how one finds the area of other shapes might help students begin to think about strategies for finding the area of a circle.

> We have found perimeters, circumferences, and areas for several shapes. Name a shape, and tell us how you would find the perimeter and area of that shape.

On the board, record the name of the shape and the rules for finding its perimeter and area. Collect information until at least rectangles, squares, parallelograms, triangles, and circles have been discussed.

Rectangle

Perimeter: Add the lengths of the four sides, or add the lengths of two touching sides and multiply by 2. In symbols this is $P = l + w + l + w$, $P = 2 \times (l + w)$, or $P = 2 \times l + 2 \times w$.

Area: Multiply the length by the width. In symbols, this is $A = l \times w$.

Square

Perimeter: Add the lengths of the four sides, or multiply the length of one side by 4. In symbols, this is $P = s + s + s + s$, or $P = 4 \times s$.

Area: Multiply the length of a side by itself. In symbols, this is $A = s \times s$, or $A = s^2$.

Parallelogram

Perimeter: Add the lengths of the four sides, or add the lengths of two touching sides and multiply by 2. In symbols, this is $P = a + a + b + b$, $P = 2 \times a + 2 \times b$, or $P = 2 \times (a + b)$.

Area: Multiply the base by the height. In symbols, this is $A = b \times h$.

Triangle

Perimeter: Add the lengths of the three sides. In symbols, this is $P = a + b + c$.

Area: Multiply the base by the height and take half the result. In symbols, this is $A = \frac{1}{2} \times b \times h$.

Circle

Circumference: Multiply the diameter by π (approximately 3.14). In symbols, this is $C = \pi \times d$.

It is not important for students to present the rules exactly as they are written here. What is important is that they have a correct formula that makes sense to them. The goal is not only to have efficient methods of finding area and perimeter, but to be flexible enough to realize that their method and another's method may sound different but accomplish the same thing.

If we look at our list, we see that finding perimeters and areas for these shapes requires adding or multiplying the measures of the lengths of sides, distance between sides, or distance between a vertex and a side. For circles, we have no straight sides; only the circumference, the diameter, and the radius.

We need to think about how to use these convenient measurements of a circle, and what we already know about finding the area of some polygons, to help us find an easier way to find the area of a circle.

In Problem 7.3, you are asked to find the area of the given circle. Experiment to try to find an easier way to compute the area. If you do find an easier way, you will need to demonstrate to the class that it works and explain why it makes sense.

Before you start, let's make some measurements that are easy to make for any circle. What is the circle's diameter? (*14 units*) How did you find that? What is the circle's radius? (*7 units*) How did you find that? What is the circle's circumference? (*about 44.9 units*) How did you find that?

Now you need to find the area. We know it can be found by counting and estimating. It is fine to do that, but here you want to look for other means of finding it.

Explore

Have students work with a partner. Encourage them to think about different methods and strategies for finding the area of the circle. As you circulate, check that they are prepared to share their answers and strategies. If students are struggling, ask questions that will help them cut down on the work by using the symmetry of the circle. Some students count a quarter of the circle and multiply by 4.

Summarize

Have students share their measures and their methods. Here are some strategies students have reported.

- Luis found the area of the largest rectangle made from whole squares that he could get inside the circle. He then counted and added the squares and parts of squares that were not inside the rectangle.

- Shondra found the area of half of the circle—a semicircle—and doubled it.

- April found the area of a quarter of the circle and multiplied it by 4.

- Phalika surrounded the circle with a large square. She found the area of the large square. Then, she found the area of the region outside of the circle, but inside of the large square, by counting the grid squares and parts of grid squares. She subtracted this area from the area of the large square to get the area of the circle.

7.4 • "Squaring" a Circle

In this problem, students make squares with sides the same length as the radius of a circle and then determine how many of these "radius squares" are needed to cover the circle. They will easily see that four is too many and three too few. The goal of the problem is to help them to discover the formula for finding the area of a circle and to understand why it makes sense. In some classrooms, it may take some directive teaching during the summary to help students make the connection to the formula.

Launch

Read Problem 7.4 with the class. You may want to demonstrate how to make the radius square for one of the circles. Demonstrate that four radius squares is too much because of the extra that overhangs the circle. Challenge your students to come up with a more precise amount.

Explore

Have students cover their circles with radius squares, then work with a partner and compare answers. As you circulate, be sure they are recording their results in a table as suggested, which is organized to help them focus on the relationship between the area of the radius square and the area of the circle. Most students will fill in the "Area of circle" column by counting grid squares. Some students may realize that they can find these values by multiplying the area of a radius square by the number of radius squares needed to cover the circle.

Summarize

Have students share their strategies for finding the number of radius squares needed to cover a circle. On the next page are some strategies students have suggested.

■ Tamara covered the circle as well as she could with three radius squares that didn't overlap. She then cut off the corners of these three squares and used them to fill in the rest of the space. It took these three corners, plus a tiny part of another radius square to cover the circle.

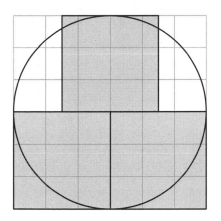

■ James covered the circle with four radius squares. He then cut off the corners of the squares and figured out how much of a radius square the corners take up. This showed that it takes four radius squares minus almost a whole radius square to cover the circle. So it takes a little more than three radius squares to cover the circle.

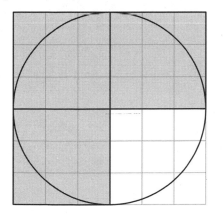

■ Su Lin used three radius square to cover three quarters of the circle. She cut off the corners of the squares, and used them to fill in the fourth quarter. This showed that it takes a little more than three radius squares to cover the circle.

On the board or overhead, create a table like the one suggested in the student edition. Ask several groups of students to fill in the table for the three circles in the problem. Add the data from some of the other circular objects that students measured.

Circle	Radius of circle	Area of radius square	Area of circle	Number of radius squares needed
1	6 units	36 square units	about 113 square units	a bit more than 3
2	4 units	16 square units	about 50.3 square units	a bit more than 3
3	3 units	9 square units	about 28.3 square units	a bit more than 3

What patterns do you notice in the data?

Students should be able to determine that it takes just over three radius squares to cover a circle. The answer, of course, is that it takes pi radius squares to cover a circle. You can help them formulate a way to describe finding the area of a circle.

1. The area of a circle is a little bit more than 3 times the area of a square that has the circle's radius as its side length.

2. The area of the radius square is found by multiplying the length by the width, which is the radius times the radius, $r \times r$ or r^2.

3. The area of a circle is thus (a little bit more than 3) $\times r \times r$ or (a little bit more than 3) $\times r^2$.

Where have we seen "a little bit more than 3" before? (*when finding circumferences of circles*) What did "a little bit more than 3" turn out to be? (*3.14, or pi*)

If we use 3.14 to calculate the area of the three circles in Problem 7.4, what do we get? (*113.04 cm², 50.24 cm², and 28.26 cm²*)

Are these areas close to what we figured before? Did anyone check our calculations by counting squares?

If I have a circle with a radius of 10 centimeters, what do you think the area of that circle is? (*314 cm²*) Explain how you got your answer.

If I have a circle with a diameter of 10 centimeters, what is the area of that circle? (*78.5 cm²*) Explain your answer.

If I have a circle with a diameter of 10 centimeters, what is its circumference? (*31.4 cm*) Explain your answer.

If I know the area of a circle, how can I find the radius and the diameter?

This question may be difficult for students, but it is worth asking. They may find r^2 and then struggle to figure how to determine the radius from that number.

7.5 • Replacing Trees

This problem gives students a chance to use their knowledge of areas of circles to investigate a real-world problem. You may want to explain the idea of a cross-section of a tree trunk.

Launch

Read the problem with the class. Make sure students understand the two replacement rules.

Explore

Have students work on the problem and follow-up in groups of three or four. As you visit the groups, remind them that they must offer an explanation for their choice and give mathematical reasons why they chose one rule over the other. If groups are having trouble, suggest that they trace the diagram from the book onto grid paper and draw a picture of what it would mean to follow each of the rules.

Summarize

Have groups share their answers and strategies for parts A and B and their responses to the follow-up. Challenge them to offer better explanations than simply, "If you want more trees in your neighborhood, the area rule is better." Have them talk about the fact that, in the given example, the area rule will provide four times as many new trees as the diameter rule. Some students may talk about the cost of the trees and say that it is not fair to make someone come up with the money necessary to buy all the trees necessary to satisfy the area model.

Additional Answers

Answer to Problem 7.1 Follow-Up

Answers will vary. Some will suggest that, since we want the most pizza for our money, it makes sense to price the pizzas according to their area. Finding the amount (area) per dollar is a good way to make comparisons. With calculators, students can find this rate by dividing the cost into the area. By area, the pizzas cost the following:

Small pizza: $\frac{63.6}{6}$ = 10.6 square inches for $1.00

Medium pizza: $\frac{113.1}{9}$ = 12.6 squares inches for $1.00

Large pizza: $\frac{176.7}{12}$ = 14.7 square inches for $1.00

Answers to Problem 7.2 Follow-Up

3. Using 3.14, the circumferences of the pizzas are 28.26 inches, 37.68 inches, and 47.1 inches. Students probably will not get these exact answers. Their answers should be somewhat close to the answers they got in Problem 7.1.

Answers to Problem 7.4

A.

Circle	Radius of circle	Area of radius square	Area of circle	Number of radius squares needed
1	6 units	36 square units	about 113 square units	a bit more than 3
2	4 units	16 square units	about 50.3 square units	a bit more than 3
3	3 units	9 square units	about 28.3 square units	a bit more than 3

Answers to Problem 7.4 Follow-Up

1. To find the area, find the radius (if you are given the diameter, divide it in half to get the radius) and the area of a radius square. The area of the circle is the area of the radius square times 3.14. We can write this in symbols as $A = 3.14 \times r^2$.

2. To find the radius, divide the area by 3.14 to get the area of a radius square. Then find a number whose square is the area of the radius square. This is the same as finding the square root of the area of the radius square. The result is the radius. To find the diameter, just double the radius.

ACE Answers

Connections

16c. The 360-sided polygon is very close to the shape of a circle. Since the turtle is traveling the "diameter" of the "circle," the problem is to find the diameter of a circle with a circumference of 360 turtle steps. Since the circumference is about 3 times the diameter, the turtle takes approximately $\frac{360}{3} = 120$ turtle steps. Students who use a value for π will obtain an answer nearer 115.

17b. The rectangle with the greatest area is a square with sides of 15 cm. Its area is 225 cm².

17c. The triangle with the greatest area is an equilateral triangle with sides of 20 cm. Its area is about 173.2 cm².

17d. The area of a regular octagon with a perimeter of 60 cm will have a larger area than the triangle, square, and hexagon. Its area is about 272 cm².

17e. If the perimeter is held at 60 cm and the number of sides of the polygon increases, the area will continue to increase.

17f. It will eventually resemble a circle. The area of a circle with a circumference of 60 cm is about 286.6 cm². A circle will enclose a maximum area for a perimeter of 60 cm.

Assigning the Unit Project

Plan a Park is the final assessment for *Covering and Surrounding*. The project gives students an opportunity to think about the amount of area things occupy. They will need to use measurement skills, concepts of area and perimeter, and reasoning about size and space to create their design.

This project could be assigned as an individual, partner, or small-group project. Assign the project near the end of the unit (during or after Investigation 7). Although this project will take several hours to complete, most of the work could be done outside of class. You may want to take 15 to 20 minutes to launch the project in class and then have students finish the project as homework.

Read through the description of the unit project, which is on pages 82 and 83 of the student edition, with the class. Make sure everyone understands the project, including the idea that Dr. Doolittle is not asking that the park be divided into two parts, but that half the total area be reserved for what she has specified. The elements she requires—the playground area, the picnic area, the trees, and the circular flower garden—can be located anywhere in the park.

Plan a Park

At the beginning of this unit, you read about Dr. Doolittle's donation of land to the city, which she designated as a new park. It is now time to design your plan for the piece of land. Use the information you have collected about parks, plus what you learned from your study of this unit, to prepare your final design.

Your design should satisfy the following constraints:

- The park should be rectangular with dimensions 120 yards by 100 yards.
- About half of the park should consist of a picnic area and a playground, but these two sections need not be located together.
- The picnic area should contain a circular flower garden. There should also be a garden in at least one other place in the park.
- There should be trees in several places in the park. Young trees will be planted, so your design should show room for the trees to grow.
- The park must appeal to families, so there should be more than just a picnic area and a playground.

Your design package should be neat, clear, and easy to follow. Your design should be drawn and labeled in black and white. In addition to a scale drawing of your design for the park, your project should include a report that gives:

1. the size (dimensions) of each item. These items should include gardens, trees, picnic tables, playground equipment, and anything else you included in your design.
2. the amount of land needed for each item and the calculations you used to determine the amount of land needed.

See the Assessment
Resources section for
detailed information about
assigning and assessing the
project, a scoring rubric,
and sample projects.

3. the materials needed. Include the amount of each item needed and the calculations you did to determine the amounts. Include the number and type of each piece of playground equipment, the amount of fencing, the numbers of picnic tables and trash containers, the amount of land covered by concrete or blacktop (so the developers can determine how much cement or blacktop will be needed), and the quantities of other items you included in your park.

4. a letter to Dr. Doolittle explaining why she should choose your design for the park. Include a justification for the choices you made about the size and quantity of items in your park.

Assessment Resources

Name _____ Date _____

1. The squares on this grid are 1 centimeter long and 1 centimeter wide. Outline two different figures with an area of 12 square centimeters and a perimeter of 16 centimeters.

2. a. On grid paper, sketch all the rectangles that can be made from exactly 16 square tiles.
   b. What do all of your rectangles have in common?

   c. How are your rectangles different?

3. a. On grid paper, sketch all the rectangles with a perimeter of 16 units that can be made from square tiles.
   b. What do all of your rectangles have in common?

   c. How are your rectangles different? Explain.

4. Are the rectangles you sketched in questions 2 and 3 the same or different? Explain your answer.

Quiz A

1. Angela works as an intern with the Department of National Resources. She is working on a study of the wildlife in a marsh near San Francisco Bay. Angela has to figure out how the marsh has changed from 1990 to 1995. Statistics are computed on the marsh every 5 years. Here are aerial maps of the marsh in 1990 and in 1995.

Marsh in 1990

Marsh in 1995

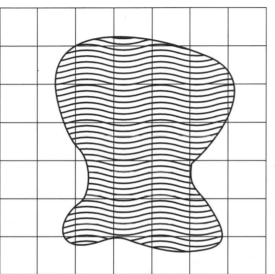

Scale

 1 mile

a. Find the approximate area and perimeter of the marsh in 1990 and in 1995.

1990 area: _____   1995 area: _____

1990 perimeter: _____   1995 perimeter: _____

b. Describe your methods for determining the area measurements in part a.

c. Do you think your estimates are too high or two low? Explain.

d. Try to imagine what may have caused changes in the marsh over the 5 years. Record your ideas.

Quiz A

2. Suppose you built all the rectangles possible from 48 square tiles.
   a. Describe the rectangle that would have the largest perimeter.

   Dimensions: _____ Perimeter: _____

   b. Describe the rectangle that would have the smallest perimeter.

   Dimensions: _____ Perimeter: _____

3. Suppose you used square tiles to build all the rectangles possible with a perimeter of 48 units.
   a. Describe the rectangle that would have the largest area.

   Dimensions: _____ Area: _____

   b. Describe the rectangle that would have the smallest area.

   Dimensions: _____ Area: _____

4. Houses, trailers, and apartments come in many different sizes and shapes. On grid paper, design a floor plan, complete with window and door locations, that covers 800 square feet. Your plan should represent a reasonable use of space for a house, apartment, or trailer. Mark on your plan the inside walls that separate the rooms. Make an organized list of all the rooms, giving their purpose, dimensions, and area.

Check-Up 2

In 1–5, calculate the area and perimeter of the figure.

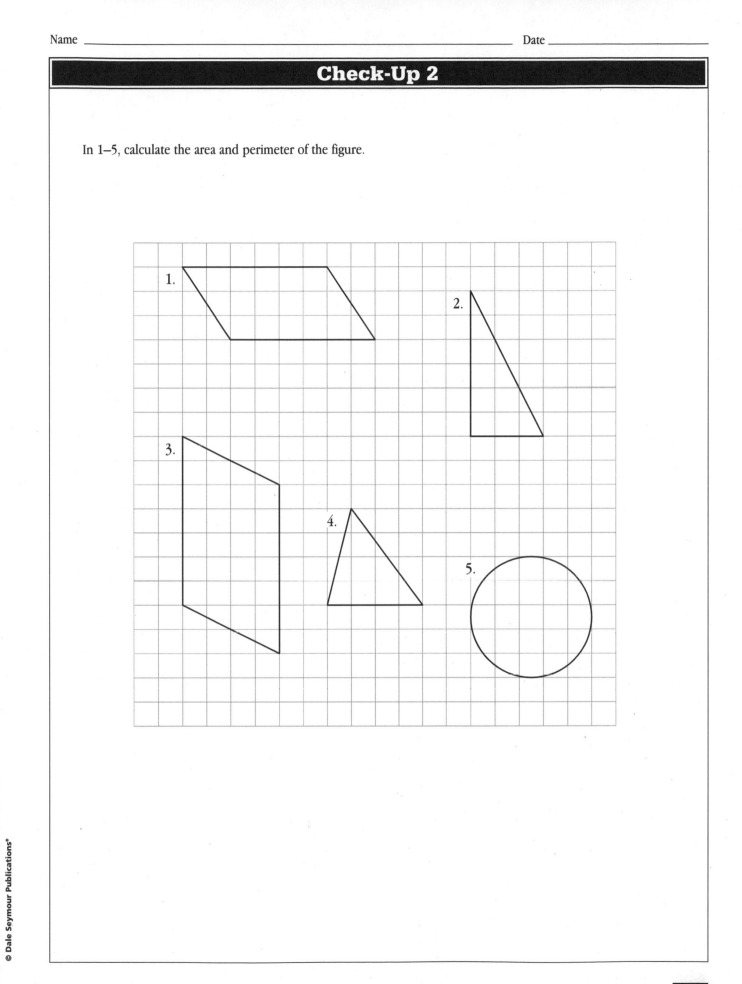

Check-Up 2

In 6–8, use what you learned in this unit to determine the area of the figure in square centimeters.

6.

7.

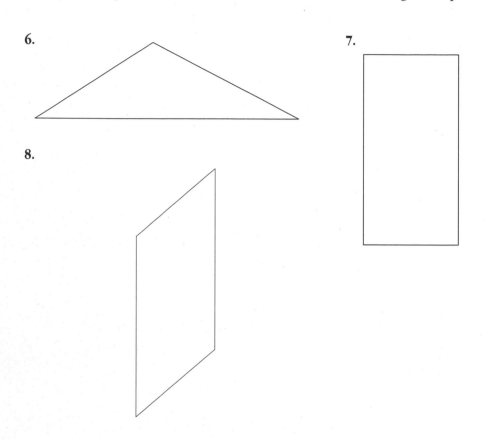

8.

9. You and two friends decide to go to the Pizza Nook for dinner. They have the best cheese pizzas in the neighborhood.

Pizza Nook Cheese Pizzas	
6-inch round pizza	$3.00
12-inch round pizza	$8.00
18-inch round pizza	$12.00

a. If you buy a 6-inch pizza, how many square inches of pizza will you get?

b. If you buy a 12-inch pizza, how many square inches of pizza will you get?

c. If you buy an 18-inch pizza, how many square inches of pizza will you get?

Quiz B

1. You may recall that the Pizza Nook sells great cheese pizzas for the following prices.

Pizza Nook Cheese Pizzas	
6-inch round pizza	$3.00
12-inch round pizza	$8.00
18-inch round pizza	$12.00

    a. How many 6-inch pizzas contain the same amount of pizza as one 12-inch pizza?

    b. How many 6-inch pizzas contain the same amount of pizza as one 18-inch pizza?

    c. The new manager of the Pizza Nook is thinking about changing the prices of cheese pizzas. It appears to him that he could think about the pricing in three ways:

    Method 1: The price of a pizza could be based on its diameter.
    Method 2: The price of a pizza could be based on its circumference.
    Method 3: The price of a pizza could be based on its area.

    If you were the manager, which method would you use to price the pizzas? Explain your reasoning.

Quiz B

2. Consider the following figures.

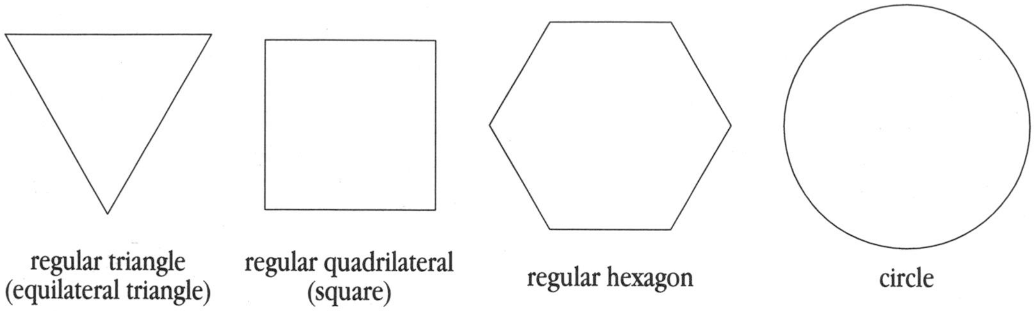

regular triangle
(equilateral triangle)   regular quadrilateral
(square)   regular hexagon   circle

Suppose each figure has a perimeter of 24 centimeters.

a. What is the length of the edges for each polygon?

Triangle: _____

Quadrilateral: _____

Hexagon: _____

b. What is the diameter of the circle?

c. Which figure has the greatest area? Explain how you arrived at your answer.

Assign these questions as additional homework, or use them as review, quiz, or test questions. Grid paper, tiles, and transparent grids can be used as needed.

Quiz

1. Jason is planning to redecorate his bedroom. He measured the room and made this rough sketch.

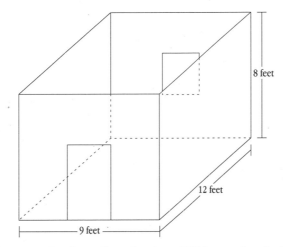

8 feet

12 feet

9 feet

a. Jason is planning to buy paint for the walls and ceiling. Will he need to find perimeter or area to figure out how much paint to buy? What unit of measure should he use?

b. To determine how much new carpet to buy, will Jason need to find perimeter or area? What unit of measure should he use?

c. Jason also needs baseboard for around the bottom of the walls. Will he need to find perimeter or area to figure out how much baseboard to buy? What unit of measure should he use?

d. How much carpeting does Jason need? Show how you found your answer.

e. How much baseboard does Jason need? Show how you found your answer.

f. If a gallon of paint covers 350 square feet, how much paint does Jason need for the walls and ceiling?

2. Chad's dad wants to repaint the top of the step outside the front door with special paint that doesn't get slippery in the rain. Below is a drawing of the top of the step. Each centimeter represents 1 foot.

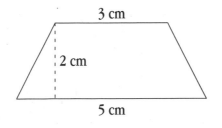

3 cm

2 cm

5 cm

a. Using the scale drawing, help Chad's dad by finding the area of the step. Keep a record of your work and sketches so you can convince him that you found it correctly.

b. Each quart of paint covers 32 square feet. Chad's dad wants to apply two coats of paint. How many quarts of paint should he buy? Explain your answer.

3. Lydia's stepmother decided to paint the semicircular patio in their back yard. Here is Lydia's sketch of the patio, drawn on a grid. Each grid square represents 1 square foot.

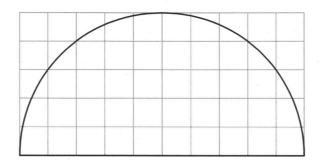

a. What is the area of the patio? Explain how you found the area.

b. Each quart of nonslip paint covers 32 square feet. How much paint should Lydia's stepmother buy if she plans to put one coat of paint on the patio? Keep a record of your work.

c. To keep grass from growing onto the patio, Lydia wants to plant a border around the patio. Since the patio is against the house, she only needs a border around the curved edge. How long will the border be? Show how you found your answer.

4. Shown below are the relative sizes of a large tile and a small tile. When measured with large tiles, the area of a rectangular room is 12 square units and the perimeter is 16 units.

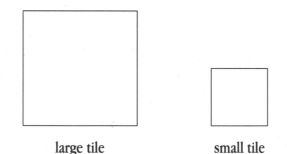

large tile   small tile

a. What would the area and perimeter of the room be (in tile units) if it were measured with the small tiles?

b. How do the measures you found in part a compare to the measures found by using the large tiles?

5. A neighbor asks you to help her design a rectangular pen for her dog, Ruff. Your neighbor has 42 meters of fencing to use for the pen.
a. What design would give Ruff the most space for playing?

b. What design would give Ruff the best space for running?

After looking at your designs, your neighbor decides to use her house as one of the walls for the pen. Her house is 35 meters long.

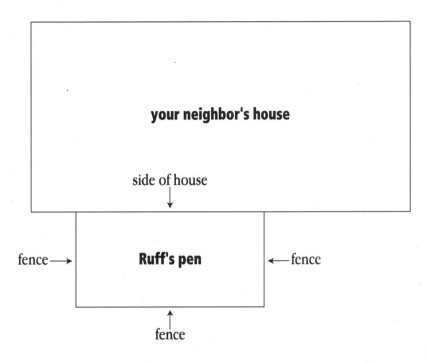

your neighbor's house

side of house

fence →   **Ruff's pen**   ← fence

fence

c. Using your neighbor's idea, now what design would give Ruff the most space for playing?

d. What design would give Ruff the best space for running?

6. The Acme sign company makes traffic signs for the state road commission. A model of the signs and their approximate measurements are given below.

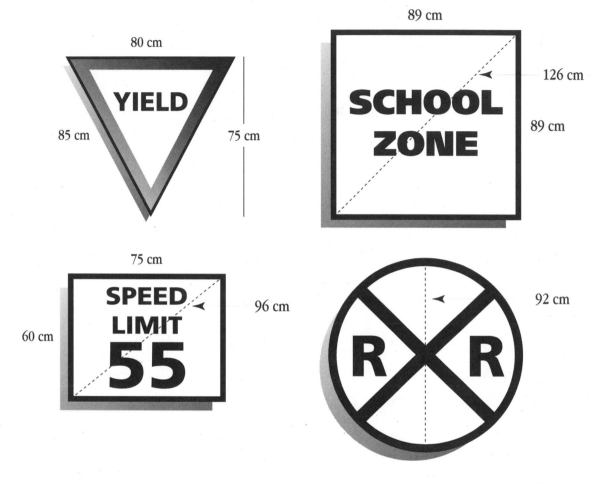

a. One of the costs that Acme must consider is the cost of metal. If metal costs $1.00 for every 1000 square centimeters, what is the cost of the metal for each sign?

Yield sign: _____

School zone sign: _____

Speed limit sign: _____

Railroad crossing sign: _____

b. After the signs are cut, the edges must be sanded to prevent metal splinters. If the cost of sanding is 2 cents for every centimeter, what will it cost to sand each sign?

Yield sign: _____

School zone sign: _____

Speed limit sign: _____

Railroad crossing sign: _____

7. Lara is helping her family build a recreation room in their basement. The room will be 28 feet by 20 feet. They have already put up the walls.

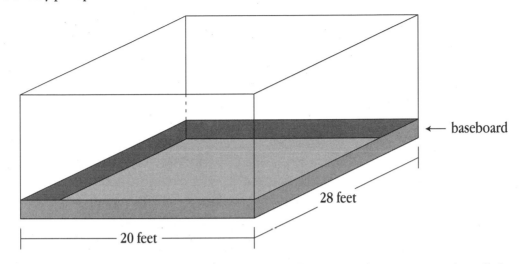

← baseboard

28 feet

20 feet

a. The family wants to tile the floor. Lara decides to buy 1-foot-square tiles. How many tiles will she need? Show your work.

b. The tiles Lara has chosen cost $0.75 each. How much will the tile floor cost? Show how you found your answer.

c. Lara needs to buy baseboard to put along the wall. How much baseboard does she need? Show how you found your answer.

d. The baseboard comes in 10-foot and 16-foot lengths. How many boards of each length should Lara buy? Show how you found your answer.

When you encounter problems like this in the real world, you will often have to consider several factors. Questions e–g look at conditions that Lara might think are important.

e. Suppose these are the prices of the baseboard.

Baseboard	
16-foot lengths	$1.25 per foot
10-foot lengths	$1.10 per foot

How many boards of each length should Lara buy if she wants to spend the least amount of money? Explain your answer.

f. When two sections of baseboard meet, they create a *seam*.

seam

If Lara wants as few seams as possible, how many baseboards of each length should she buy?

g. If you were Lara, how many baseboards of each length would you buy?

Name _____ Date _____

1. Find the perimeter and area of each figure below. Explain your strategy for finding each answer.

    a.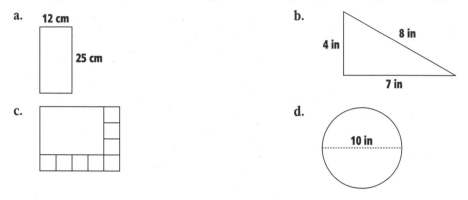
    12 cm
    25 cm

    b.
    8 in
    4 in
    7 in

    c.

    d.
    10 in

2. Each grid square at right is 1 centimeter by 1 centimeter. Jordan says that the area of the shape on the grid is about 25 square centimeters.

    a. How do you think Jordan's estimate compares to the actual area? Explain.

    b. Find your own estimate for the area of the shape. Explain your strategy.

3. Find the perimeter and area of the parallelogram below.

    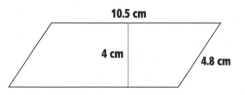
    10.5 cm
    4 cm
    4.8 cm

Unit Test

4. The table below shows lengths and widths of different rectangles.

Length	Width
1 cm	8 cm
2 cm	7 cm
3 cm	6 cm
4 cm	5 cm

   a. As you read down the table, are the areas of the rectangles constant or changing? Explain.

   b. As you read down the table, are the perimeters of the rectangles constant or changing? Explain.

5. A rectangle with an area of 30 square units has sides with whole-number lengths.

   a. Could the perimeter of the rectangle be 22 units? Explain your reasoning.

   b. Could the perimeter of the rectangle be 34 units? Explain your reasoning.

6. Find the perimeter and area of the figure below. Explain the strategy you use to find your answers.

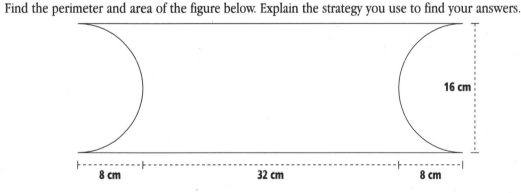

8 cm   32 cm   8 cm

16 cm

7. Irene drew a rectangle with an area of 196 square units. She finds that this is the largest area possible for any rectangle with the same perimeter.

   a. What are the dimensions of the rectangle? Explain your reasoning.

   b. What is the perimeter of the rectangle? Explain your reasoning.

Notebook Checklist

Journal Organization

_____ Problems and Mathematical Reflections are labeled and dated.

_____ Work is neat and easy to find and follow.

Vocabulary

_____ All words are listed.

_____ All words are defined or described.

Quizzes and Check-Ups

_____ Check-Up 1   _____ Quiz A

_____ Check-Up 2   _____ Quiz B

Homework Assignments

_____ _____

_____ _____

_____ _____

_____ _____

_____ _____

_____ _____

_____ _____

_____ _____

_____ _____

_____ _____

_____ _____

_____ _____

_____ _____

_____ _____

Self Assessment

Vocabulary

Of the vocabulary words I defined or described in my journal, the word _____ best demonstrates my ability to give a clear definition or description.

Of the vocabulary words I defined or described in my journal, the word _____ best demonstrates my ability to use an example to help explain or describe an idea.

Mathematical Ideas

1. a. I learned these things about the relationships between area and perimeter:

    b. I learned these things about how to find the area and perimeter of rectangles, parallelograms, triangles, and circles:

    c. Here are page numbers of journal entries that give evidence of what I have learned, along with descriptions of what each entry shows:

2. a. These are the mathematical ideas I am still struggling with:

    b. This is why I think these ideas are difficult for me:

    c. Here are page numbers of journal entries that give evidence of what I am struggling with, along with descriptions of what each entry shows:

Class Participation

I contributed to the classroom discussion and understanding of *Covering and Surrounding* when I . . . (Give examples.)

Answers to Check-Up 1

1. Only one rectangular arrangement is possible (a 6 × 2), but several nonrectangular figures are possible. Figures must have an area of 12 square centimeters and a perimeter of 16 centimeters. Possible answer:

2. **a.**

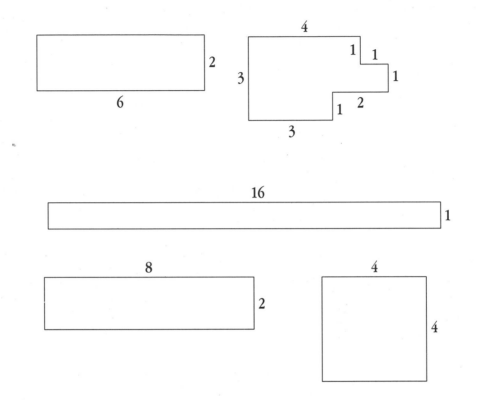

   b. They are all rectangles and thus have four sides, opposite sides equal, and four right angles; and they all have an area of 16 square units.

   c. The lengths of the sides are different and thus the rectangles have different perimeters.

3. **a.**

Answer Keys

    b. They are all rectangles and thus have four sides, opposite sides equal, and four right angles; and they all have a perimeter of 16 units.

    c. They have different side lengths, so the number of tiles in a row and the number of rows of tiles are different, giving them different areas.

4. The rectangles are different—except for one, the 4×4 rectangle—because they are filling different requirements. Question 2 asked for rectangles with an area of 16 square units, and question 3 asked for rectangles with a perimeter of 16 units. These are two different measures and give two different sets of rectangles. Only the 4×4 rectangle meets both requirements.

Answers to Quiz A

1.   **a.** 1990: area = about 32 to 33 square miles, perimeter = about 23 to 25 miles
       1995: area = about 20 square miles, perimeter = about 19 to 21 miles

    b. Answers will vary. Most students will count whole squares and combine partial squares to determine area. Some may find the area of the grid and subtract the amount not covered by the marsh. To find perimeter, many students will encircle the area with string and then measure the string. Some may estimate the marsh edge within each square, deciding whether each edge is greater than or less than a centimeter (which usually proves to be an ineffective means of finding perimeter).

    c. Answers will vary. Some students may feel their estimates are accurate and explain why. Others who feel their estimates are high may explain that they counted any square half or more covered as a whole square. Those who feel their estimates are too low may explain how they ignored squares that were less than half covered.

    d. Possible explanations: drought, land development cutting off water flow, changes in irrigation

2.   **a.** dimensions: 1×48, perimeter = 98 units

    b. dimensions: 6×8, perimeter = 28 units

3.   **a.** dimensions: 12×12, area = 144 square units

    b. dimensions: 1×23, area = 23 square units

4. Answers will vary. All plans should have a total area of 800 square feet. Students often struggle with this question. Some may present plans with rooms that are unreasonable (bathrooms with 2 square feet of space, closets with 1 square foot of space). If your students have such difficulties, you may wish to discuss the problem in class, marking off some of their suggested rooms on the floor of the classroom and asking if the sizes are reasonable.

Answers to Check-Up 2

1. area = 18 square units, perimeter = about 19.2 units

2. area = 9 square units, perimeter = about 15.7 units

3. area = 28 square units, perimeter = about 22.9 units

4. area = 8 square units, perimeter = about 13.1 units

5. area = 19.6 square units (using $A = \pi r^2$), perimeter = about 15.7 units (using $P = \pi d$)

6. area = 7 cm²

7. area = 12.5 cm²

8. area = about 9.4 cm²

9. **a.** about 28.3 square inches

    b. about 113.1 square inches

    c. about 254.5 square inches

Answers to Quiz B

1. This question requires students to compare the area of a small pizza to that of a medium and large pizza. Students found the areas for these pizzas in Check-Up 2.

    a. $113.1 \div 28.3 = 4$ six-inch pizzas

    b. $254.5 \div 28.3 = 9$ six-inch pizzas

    c. Possible answer: Method 3; The amount of ingredients in a pizza is best reflected by its area rather than its diameter or circumference. It may be somewhat misleading to students that round pizzas are usually described by their diameter.

2. **a.** triangle = 8 cm, quadrilateral = 6 cm, hexagon = 4 cm

    b. about 7.6 cm

    c. the circle; Possible explanation: I found the area of all the figures and compared them: the area of the triangle is about 27 cm², the area of the square is 36 cm², the area of the hexagon is about 42 cm², and the area of the circle is about 45.34 cm².

Answers to the Question Bank

1. **a.** area, square feet

    b. area, square yards (or square feet)

    c. perimeter, feet

    d. The room is 3 yards (9 feet) by 4 yards (12 feet), so $3 \times 4 = 12$ square yards of carpet are needed (108 square feet is also correct).

    e. $(9 + 12) \times 2 = 42$ feet of baseboard (Some students may argue for less than 42 feet—say, 39 feet—because of the door opening not needing baseboard. This is a reasonable answer as well.)

    f. Possible answer: Two of the walls need $12 \times 8 = 96$ square feet of paint, two of the walls need $9 \times 8 = 72$ square feet of paint, and the ceiling needs $12 \times 9 = 108$ square feet of paint, so there is $(96 \times 2) + (72 \times 2) + 108 = 444$ square feet to cover. This would require $444 \div 350 =$ about 1.27 gallons of paint, so you would need $1\frac{1}{2}$ or 2 gallons (if the paint came only in full gallons).

2. **a.** Some students may know that the formula for the area of a trapezoid is $\frac{(b_1 + b_2)}{2} \times h$ and calculate $\frac{(3 + 5)}{2} \times 2 = 8$ square feet. Others may divide the trapezoid into a rectangle and two triangles, where the area of the rectangle is $3 \times 2 = 6$ square feet and the area of each congruent triangle is $2 \times 1 \div 2 = 1$ square foot for a total of $6 + 1 + 1 = 8$ square feet.

   b. For two coats he needs to cover $8 \times 2 = 16$ square feet. A quart covers 32 square feet, and 16 is half of 32, so half a quart of paint is needed. If you can't buy the paint in half quarts, 1 quart would be needed.

3.   **a.** area = about 39.3 square feet

   b. For one coat she needs to cover 39.3 square feet A quart covers 32 square feet, and $39.3 \div 32 =$ about 1.2 quarts. If the paint only comes in full quarts, 2 quarts would be needed. If you can buy the paint in half quarts, $1\frac{1}{2}$ quarts would be needed.

   c. For a circle, the border would be $3.14 \times 10 = 31.4$ feet. For a semicircle, the border will be $31.4 \div 2 = 15.7$ feet

4.   **a.** In small tile units, the area would be 48 square units and the perimeter would be 32 units.

   b. Since it takes four small tiles to equal the area of one large tile, the area in small tile units is four times the area in large tile units. Since it takes two small tile edges to equal the length of one large tile edge, the perimeter in small tile units is twice the perimeter in large tile units.

5.   **a.** The idea here is to find the pen with the largest area. If students use whole units, the pen with the largest area is a 10×11 rectangle. A more sophisticated answer would take into account the fact that whole units are not a restriction; thus the pen with the largest area would be a 10.5×10.5 square.

   b. The idea here is to find the pen with the longest running area. The longest and thinnest design using whole-number units is a 20×1 rectangular pen. Some students might argue for other sizes, such as a 19×2 pen, to give the dog more room to turn around.

   c. If students use whole units, the pen could have fence side lengths of 10, 22, and 10 meters or 11, 20, and 11 meters which, with the house as the fourth side of the pen, results in an area of 220 square meters. A more sophisticated answer would involve considering rational numbers; the pen could have side lengths of 10.5, 21, and 10.5 meters and an area of 220.5 square meters.

   d. Students might argue for a 3.5×35 meter pen because the house (which is 35 meters long) is to be one side on the pen and that leaves 7 meters for the two short ends. Others might argue that you could use the fencing to extend the house wall and suggest a 1.5×37 meter pen or a 1×37.5 meter pen.

6.   **a.** yield sign: area = 3000 square centimeters, so cost = $3.00

      school zone sign: area = 7921 square centimeters, so cost = $7.92

      speed limit sign: area = 4500 square centimeters, so cost = $4.50

      railroad crossing sign: area = about 6647.6 square centimeters, so cost = $6.65

   b. yield sign: perimeter = 250 centimeters, so cost = $5.00

      school zone sign—perimeter = 356 centimeters, so cost = $7.12

      speed limit sign—perimeter = 270 centimeters, so cost = $5.40

      railroad crossing sign—circumference = 288.9 centimeters, so cost = $5.78

7.   **a.** The area of the floor is $28 \times 20 = 560$ square feet, so Lara needs 560 floor tiles.

   b. $560 \times 0.75 = 420$, so the tiles will cost $420.

   c. The perimeter of the room is $(28 + 20) \times 2 = 96$ feet, so Lara needs 96 feet of baseboard.

   d. Possible answer: Since $96 \div 16 = 6$, Lara could buy six 16-foot lengths of baseboard.

e. The 10-foot lengths are a better buy, so Lara should buy as many of those as possible. She could buy eight 10-foot lengths and one 16-foot length ($8 \times 10 + 16 = 96$).

f. Possible answers: Lara could buy four 10-foot boards (two for each of the shorter walls) and four 16-foot boards (two for each of the longer walls). Lara could buy six 16-foot boards, use two for each of the longer walls and use one 16-foot board plus the 4-foot length left over from the longer walls for each of the shorter walls. Each of these configurations would produce a seam at each corner and one on each wall.

g. Answers will vary. They should represent a reasonable tradeoff between price and number of seams.

Answers to the Unit Test

1. a. P = 74 cm, A = 300 sq. cm
   b. P = 19 cm, A = 14 sq. cm
   c. P = 18 units, A = 20 sq. units
   d. P = 31.4 in, A = 78.5 sq. in

2. a. Jordan's estimate is too small because 25 sq. cm is just the area of the whole squares inside the shape and does not include the additional area of the partial squares that are inside the shape.

   b. A closer estimate to the actual area of the shape would be 32 sq. cm which can be found by "piecing together" whole grid squares from the partial squares that are inside the shape.

3. P = 30.6 cm, A = 42 sq. cm

4. a. The areas of the rectangles increase going down the rows of the table:
   8 sq. cm, 14 sq. cm, 18 sq. cm, and 20 sq. cm

   b. The perimeter of the rectangles is constant, P = 18 cm.

5. a. Yes, for a 5×6 rectangle A = 30 sq. units and P = 22 units.

   b. Yes, for a 2×15 rectangle A = 30 sq. units and P = 34 units.

6. See the figure as having two curved sides that together make a circle of radius 8.
   P = 48 + 48 + 16π = 96 + (16 × 3.14) = 146.26 cm
   A = (16 × 48) − 64π = 768 − 201.06 = 566.94 sq. cm

7. a. The largest rectangle for a fixed perimeter is a square, and so Irene's rectangle would be a square with a side length of 14 (and $14 \times 14 = 196$ sq. cm).

   b. The perimeter of the rectangle would be $4 \times 14 = 56$ cm.

Plan a Park is the final assessment in *Covering and Surrounding*. The project was introduced at the beginning of the unit. Students were told about a contest to design the layout of a city park. After each investigation, students were reminded to think about the concepts they were learning and how they might use these ideas in their park designs. They were also asked to visit local parks or school playgrounds and make measurements of things they might put in their designs.

Plan a Park gives students an opportunity to think about the size of things and the amount of area they occupy. They will need to use measurement skills, concepts of area and perimeter, ideas of scaling, and reasoning about size and space to create their designs.

The project could be assigned as an individual or partner project. An ample supply of grid paper, as well as calculators, rulers, measuring tapes, string, and compasses should be available for students to use as they conduct research for their park designs. (Grid paper on large rolls is available through teacher-supply catalogs or stores.) We recommend that students use grid paper with small squares because of the size of the park.

Read through the description of the unit project, which is on pages 82 and 83 of the student edition. Make sure everyone understands the project, including the idea that Dr. Doolittle is not asking that the park be divided into two parts, but that *half of the total area* be reserved for what she has specified. The elements she requires—the playground, the picnic area, the trees, and the circular flower garden—can be located anywhere in the park.

You will want to talk with your students about what it means to make a scale drawing. You could discuss how to set up a one-to-one scale with grid paper. For example, if students will be using centimeter grid paper, one centimeter on the grid paper could represent one yard of the park. Your students have been informally making scale drawings through out the unit, beginning with the tile models of bumper car floors. Because the audience for the design is more than the teacher, each design should include a key that gives the scaling ratio.

Although this project will take several hours to complete, most of the work can be done outside of class. You may want to take 10 or 15 minutes to launch the project in class and then a few minutes every couple of days to discuss questions your students have as they work on their projects. A week, including a weekend, is a reasonable amount of time to give students for this project.

Here are some common questions that students ask, along with suggested answers:

Q: How do I represent trees? Do I show the trunk or the spread of the branches?
A: Most landscape drawings are aerial views, so you should show the spread of the branches.

Q: Do I have to show calculations for the numbers of trees and picnic tables?
A: No, you can just find these by counting. You need to include the counts for these items, but not an addition equation to show the sum of the tables and the trees.

Q: Do I have to give the perimeter *and* the area for each item in my park?

A: No, you should be selective about the measurements you include. For example, when you describe the amount of fencing needed for your park, you need only give perimeter. When you specify the amount of space needed for the picnic area, you need only give area.

Remind students that their reports should be organized so the reader can easily find information about items in the park. Giving students your grading rubric for the project should help them understand what they need to do.

Suggested Scoring Rubric

A total of 50 points is possible for the project—23 for the scale drawing, 22 for the report, and 5 for the letter to Dr. Doolittle.

Scale drawing

Dimensions and measurements—16 points
- dimensions are labeled (3 pts)
- dimensions are close to dimensions of actual items (9 pts)
- scale is included (2 pts)
- design meets problem constraints (2 pts)

Complete design—7 points
- design is reasonable and logical (4 pts)
- design is neat, well-organized, and includes required items (3 pts)

Report

Mathematics—16 points
- dimensions are given and correctly match drawing (4 pts)
- calculations are correct (6 pts)
- necessary and correct measurements are given with explanations of what the measurements mean and why they are needed (6 pts)

Organization—6 points
- work is neat, easy to follow, and meets the requirements of the problem (3 pts)
- information is easy to find (3 pts)

Letter

Composition—3 points
- letter is easy to read and understand (1 pt)
- justifications are given for decisions (1 pt)
- reasons are given for why design should be chosen (1 pt)

Structure—2 points
- letter is neat (1 pt)
- grammar and spelling are correct (1 pt)

Sample

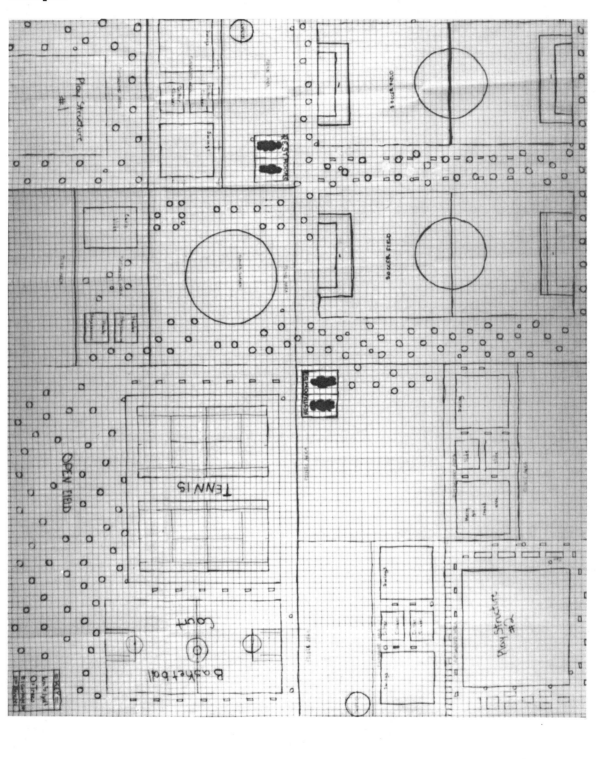

Dear D. Dolittle,

Our park was designed to ~~make~~ have families come and be able to spend a day outdoors together. We have a basketball court and tennis court in the top left corner and two soccer fields in the lower right corner. We included the sports fields so people can play for fun or the community can use the fields and courts for matches and tournaments.

To the left of our soccer fields we have picnic and playground areas. There are many fun and exciting play structures, climbers, swings and much more. We have covered the ground of our playground with sand for safety.

We have conveniently located benches around the sports fields so parents can sit down and relax while they watch their son or daughter play. This way they won't have to bring their own chairs. We have added restrooms in the center so they can be used by anyone in the park. We

also added both garbage and recycling, ~~cans~~ cans for a clean park.

Our park meets all your constraints, has something for everyone, is ecologically minded with recycling and trees and will be a fun place for the family. We hope you will select our design.

Sincerely,

Katie
Rebecca

Land Used

2 soccer fields
    21yd by 45yd
    945 yd² area
    132 yd perimeter

2 tennis courts
    12yd x 22yd
    264 yd² area
    68 yd perimeter

basketball
    16yd x 30yd
    480 yd² area
    92 yd perimeter

Total land used for soccer, tennis and basketball $945 + 945yd² + 264yd² + 264yd² + 480yd² =$
    $\underline{2,898}$ yd²

Playground

5 sets of swings   9yd x 9yd
                81yd² area
                36yd perimeter

4 Critter Climbers   4yd x 5yd
                20yd² area
                18yd perimeter

1 curly slide   9yd x 7yd
                63yd² area
                32yd perimeter

2 slide area   4yd x 5yd
                20yd² area
                18yd perimeter

Play structure #1   17 yd + 17 yd

289 yd² area

68 yd perimeter

Play structure #2   20 yd × 18 yd

360 yd² area

76 yd perimeter

Playground area

4   30 yd × 12.5 yd =   1,500 yd²

2   30 yd × 25 yd =   1,500 yd²

_____

3,000 yd² total

playground

Small flower gardens

diameter   4 yd

radius   2 yd
(½ D)

area   12.57 yd²

r × r × π

circumference   12.57 yd

D × π

Restrooms

6 yd × 8 yd

area   48 yd²

perimeter 28 yd

Picnic Area

4   30 yd × 12.5 yd =   1,500 yd²

2   30 yd × 25 yd =   1,500 yd²

_____

3,000 yd² total

picnic

Flower Garden

Big   diameter   16 yd

radius (½ d)   8 yd

area =   201.06 yd²

r × r × π

circumference =   50.27 yd

D × π

Cement needed

480 yd² for basketball court area

Clay   832 yd² for tennis courts

Sand   3,000 yd² for playground area

Soil for gardens

large + small gardens added = 226.2 yd²

fencing for tennis court

w + w + l + l =

32 yd + 32 yd + 26 yd + 26 yd = 116 yd

benches   1 yd by ½ yd =

3 ft × 1.5 ft = 4.5 ft²

there are 88

---

trash cans

       23 trash cans

trees =
  d 1 yd
  r .5 yd
  a = .78 yd^2

Total park area = 100 yd x 126 yd = 12,000 yd

    total park   12,000 yd^2
picnic &   - 6,000 yd^2
playground   ————————
           6,000 yd^2

The total park area was 12,000 yd^2.
We subtracted the total area for the picnic and
playground which was 3,000 yd^2 + 3,000 yd^2 = 6,000 yd^2
leaving 6,000 yd^2 for other activities. We
can tell this is ½ of 12,000. There is also
open field areas around the tennis and basketball
courts. We did not subtract the flower garden
area but if we did it would equal

  3,000 yd^2 area for picnic
- 201.06 yd^2 area for garden
————————
2798.94 yd^2
+3000 yd playground area
————————
5798.94 yd^2 picnic + playground

             .483
12000 yd^2 $\overline{)5798.94 \text{ yd}^2}$ or 48%

A Teacher's Comments

In my class, students worked on the project in pairs. They put a lot of time and energy into the projects but had a hard time figuring out how to show the mathematics and organize the information. The sample project was created by a pair of students that struggled with these issues.

Scale drawing
Dimensions and measurements—9 out of 16 points
Most of the items in the design are close to the correct scaled size. One exception is the soccer field.

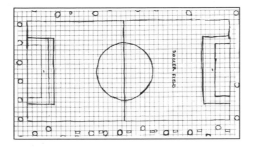

A regulation soccer field is 120 yards by 60 yards (more than half of the park). Although junior soccer fields are sometimes smaller, there is no indication that the fields in the design are junior soccer fields. The letter to Dr. Doolittle states that the community could hold tournaments on these fields, which implies that they are regulation size.

Other problems are the sizes of the swings and play structures, which are shown as square areas.

The report does not explain why these areas are squares or why they are the size that they are. Also, no explanation is given about what "play structure area" means. Because of these concerns, I gave only 5 points for close and reasonable dimensions. I gave no points for labeling the dimensions of items in the park. The students must have missed this part of the assignment. They received 2 points for the key.

The design meets the requirements that half of the park be picnic or playground area, that the picnic area include a flower garden, and that the items in the park appeal to families, so I gave 2 points for this criteria.

Complete design—6 out of 7 points
The design of the park seems reasonable, except for the size of the soccer field. One might question the fact that the picnic area has no tables or trash cans. Also, "open field" implies a piece of land with no trees or equipment, yet this drawing shows several trees in the open field.

Report
Mathematics—11 out of 16 points
Most of the dimensions in the report (other than the soccer field) match the drawing. The biggest problem is that the reader has to work hard to determine what counts as playground and picnic areas and what the dimensions are. As a result, I subtracted points for "Organization" below. The given calculations were correct (6 points), but the students do not show evidence of thinking about what these measurements are, what they mean, and why they are needed. For example, the perimeter and area of the tennis courts are given with no explanation of why they are given or what they imply for the park design. The perimeters of the tennis courts are not needed, which is evident in the calculations of the amount of fencing required for this area. By examining the numbers for these calculations, it is clear that the fence is intended to surround both tennis courts and not each individual court. I gave 2 points for necessary and correct measurements with explanations.

Organization—2 out of 6 points
The organization of the report is the weakest part of the project. Refering to the rubric, I awarded only 1 out of 3 points for "work is neat, easy to follow, and meets the requirements of the problem" and 1 out of 3 points for "information is easy to find."

Letter
Composition—3 out of 3 points
The letter was clear and attempts to justify the decisions that were made.

Structure—1 out of 2 points
The letter is not very neat and it contains crossed-out words.

I awarded 32 out of 50 points—a C—for this project. The students have addressed the basic elements of the project, but there are problems with completeness and reasonableness.

When I assign this project next time, I will need to help my students better understand what quality work is and what my expectations are. I need to help them think more about measurements and what they tell us. It is apparent that students can find areas and perimeters, but it is not clear that they are reasoning about these measures. I need to find ways to raise these issues when I teach this unit. Having students do more measuring of actual items may give them more frames of reference for size. Organizing information is a difficult task for my students. This was apparent in many of the reports turned in for this project. I need to talk more about organization with my students and model some of the ways I organize information.

Blackline Masters

ACE Question 4

Sarah's Field

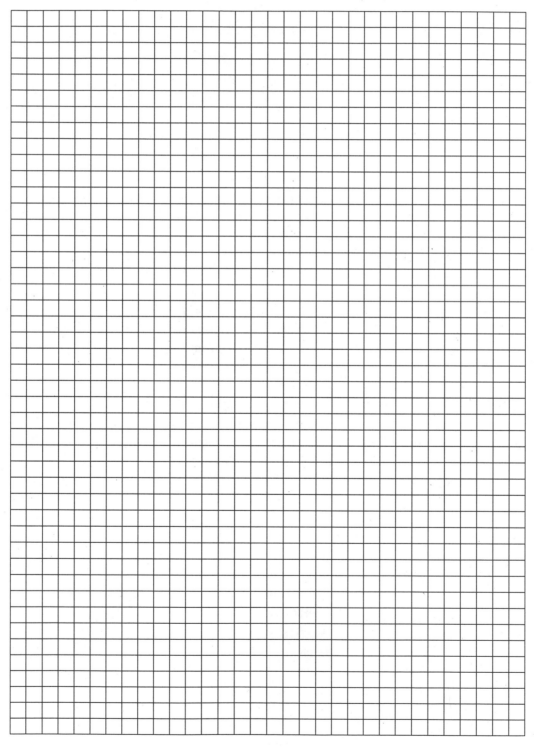

Problem 5.1 Shapes

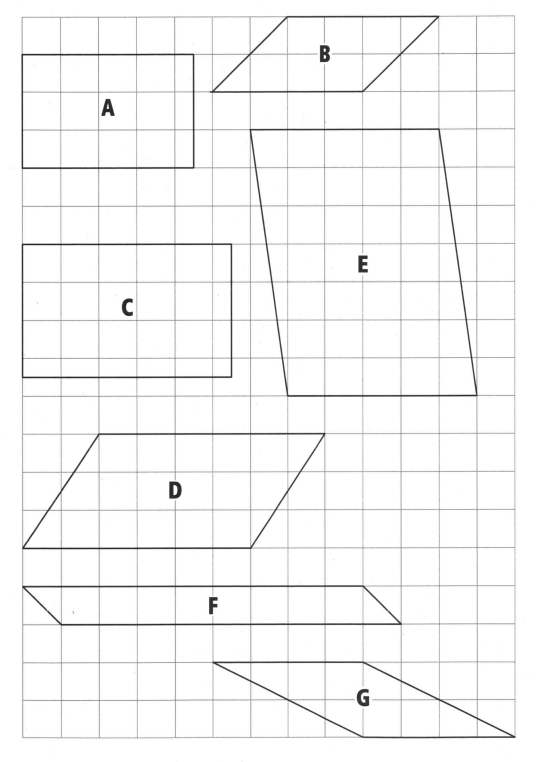

Problem 6.1 Shapes

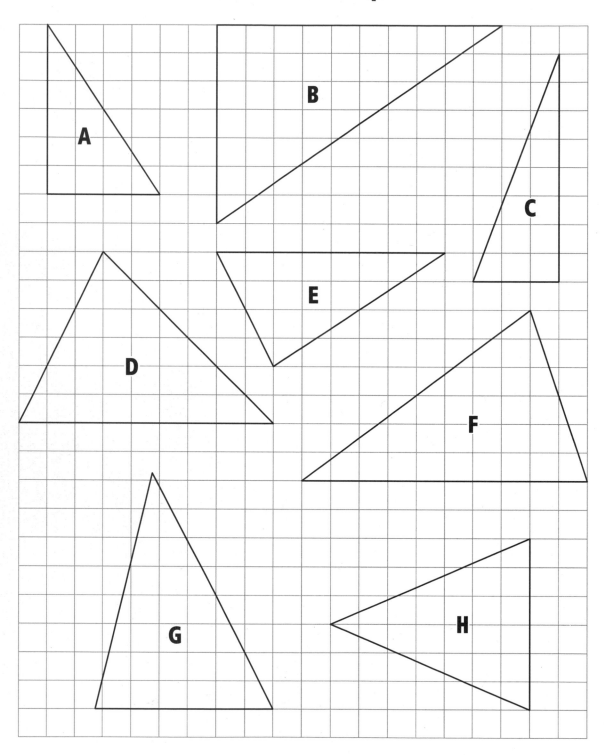

Circles and Radius Squares

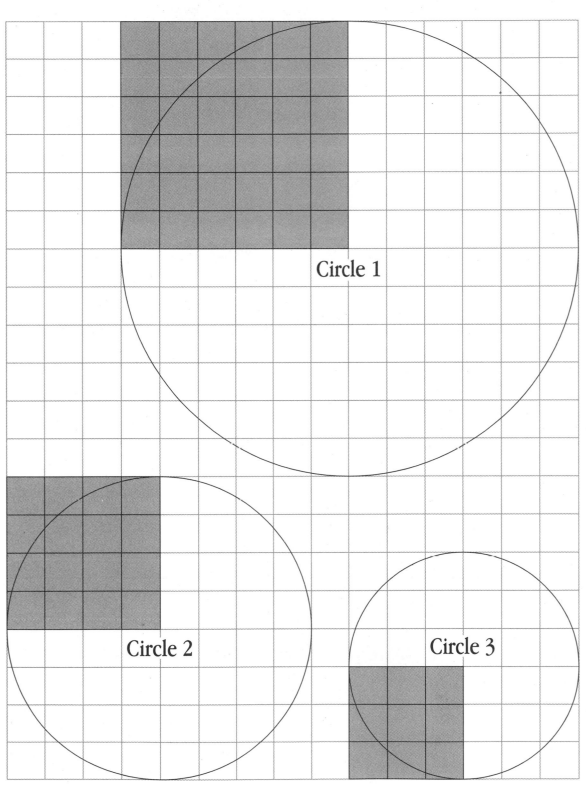

Solve these design problems by experimenting with square tiles.

A. Badger State Shows in Wisconsin requested a bumper-car ride with a total of 36 square meters of floor space and 26 rail sections. Sketch some possible designs for this floor plan.

B. Lone Star Carnivals in Texas wants a bumper-car ride that covers 36 square meters of floor space and has lots of rail sections for riders to bump against. Sketch some possible designs for this floor plan.

C. Design a bumper-car floor plan with 36 or more square meters of floor space that you think would make an interesting ride. Be prepared to share your design with the class and to explain why you like it.

Use the sample rail section and floor tile to answer these questions.

A. Which of the three designs provides the greatest floor space (has the greatest area)?

B. Which of the three designs requires the most rail sections (has the greatest perimeter)?

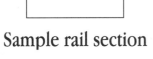

Sample rail section   Sample floor tile section

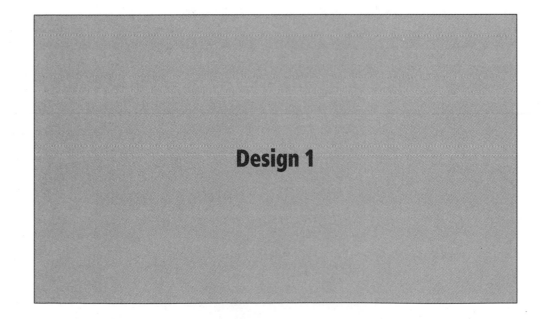

Design 1

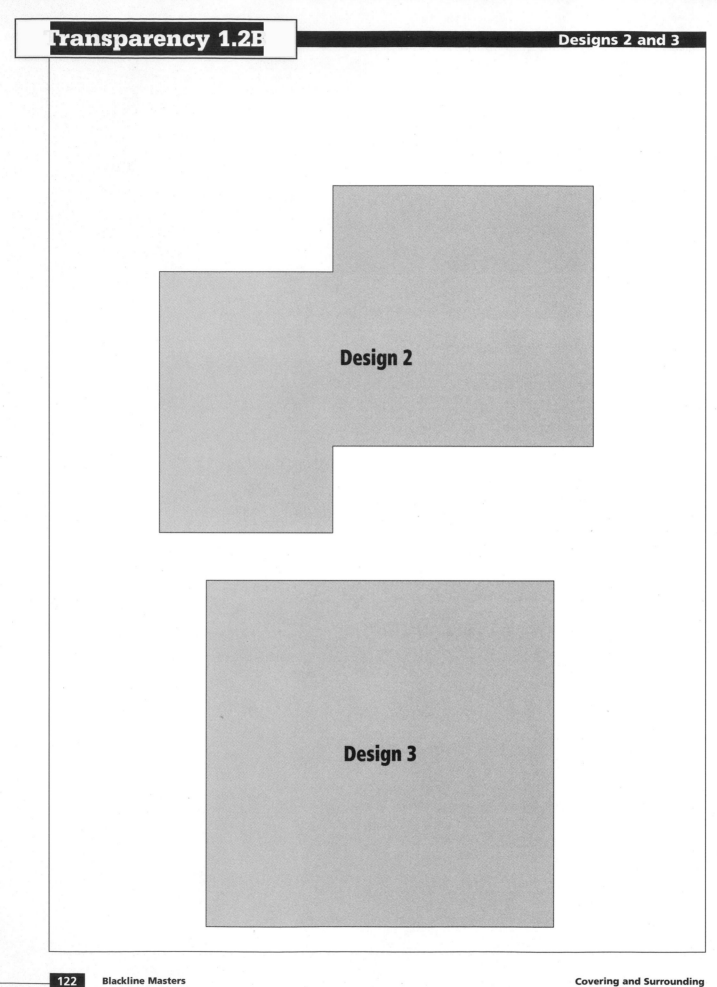

Design 2

Design 3

A. The MARs company charges $25 for each rail section and $30 for each floor tile. How much would each of the designs cost? Record your data in a table with these column headings:

Design	Area	Perimeter	Cost of tiles	Cost of rail sections	Total cost

B. If you were the buyer for Buckeye Amusements, which design would you choose? Explain your choice.

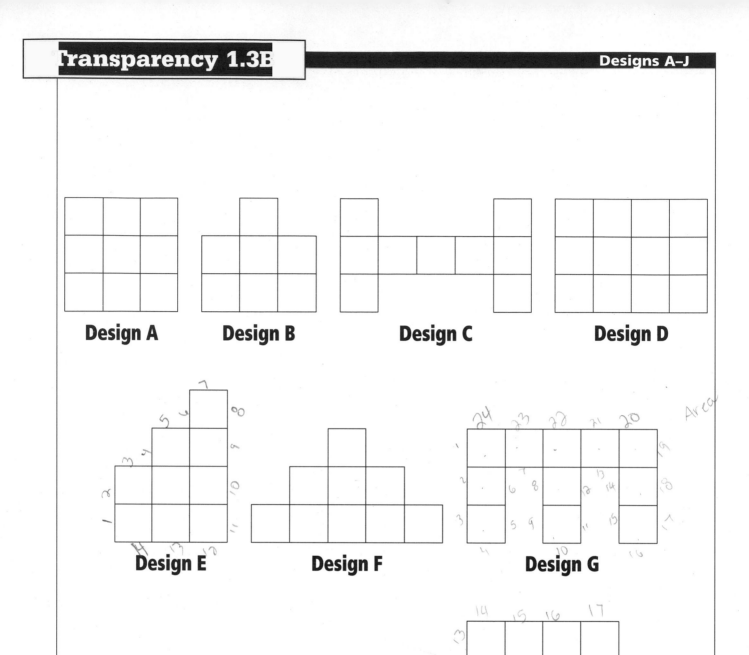

Design A   **Design B**   **Design C**   **Design D**

Design E   **Design F**   **Design G**

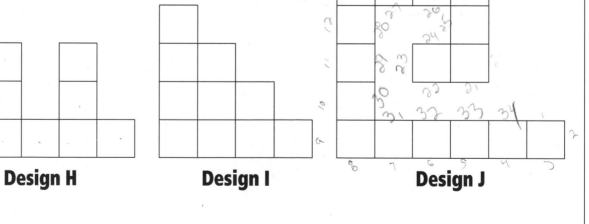

Design H   **Design I**   **Design J**

Questions A–E refer to the designs from Problem 1.3. Experiment with your tiles to try to answer the questions. Make sketches of your designs.

A. Build a design with the same area as design G, but with a smaller perimeter. Can you make more than one design that meets these requirements? Explain.

B. Design E can be made from design D by removing three tiles. How does the area of design D compare to the area of design E? How does the perimeter of design D compare to the perimeter of design E?

C. Design F and design I have the same perimeter. Can you rearrange the tiles of design F to make design I? Explain.

D. Design A and design C have the same area. Can you rearrange the tiles of design A to make design C? Explain.

E. Arrange your tiles to match design B. Now, move one tile to make a new design with a perimeter of 14 units. Sketch your new design.

With your group, have a discussion about measuring feet. In what ways can you measure a foot? Which of these measurements would be of interest to shoe companies?

Have each person in your group trace one foot on a piece of grid paper.

For each person's foot, estimate the length, width, area, perimeter, and any other measures your group thinks should be included. Record your data in a table with these column headings:

Student	Shoe size	Foot length	Foot width	Foot area	Foot perimeter

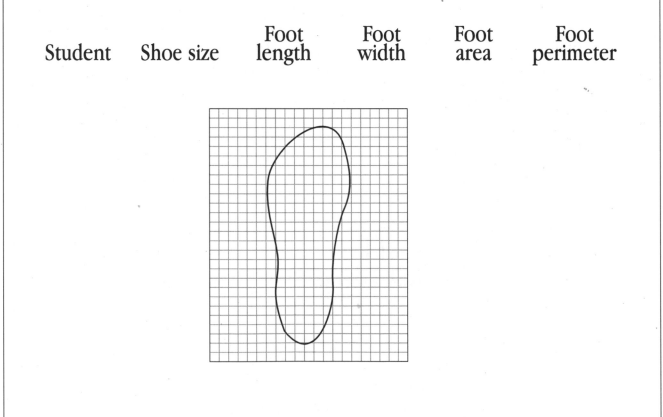

The rangers in Great Smoky Mountains National Park want to build several inexpensive storm shelters. The shelters must have 24 square meters of floor space. Suppose that the walls are made of sections that are 1 meter wide and cost $125.

A. Use your tiles to experiment with different *rectangular* shapes. Sketch each possible floor plan on grid paper. Record your group's data in a table with these column headings:

Length   Width   Perimeter   Area   Cost of walls

B. Based on the cost of the wall sections, which design would be the least expensive to build? Describe what that shelter would look like.

C. Which shelter plan has the most expensive set of wall sections? Describe what that shelter would look like.

Draw a 4×6 rectangle on grid paper, and cut it out.

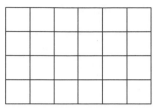

Starting at one corner, cut an interesting path to an adjacent corner.

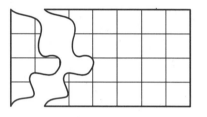

Slide the piece you cut out onto the opposite edge. Tape the two pieces together, matching the straight edges.

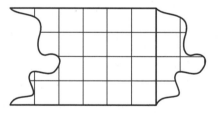

A. Find the area and the perimeter of your new figure.

B. Is the perimeter of the new figure larger than, the same as, or smaller than the perimeter of a 4×6 rectangle? Explain.

C. Could you make a figure with an area of 24 square units with a longer perimeter than you found in your first figure? Explain your answer.

Suppose you wanted to help a friend build a rectangular pen for her dog, Shane. You have 24 meters of fencing, in 1-meter lengths, to build the pen. Which rectangular shape would be best for Shane?

Experiment with your square tiles to find all possible rectangles with a *perimeter* of 24 meters. Sketch each rectangle on grid paper. Record your data about each possible plan in a table with these column headings:

Length   Width   Perimeter   Area

Make this pentomino with your tiles.

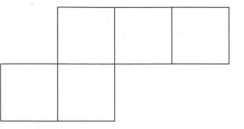

A. Add tiles to the pentomino to make a new figure with a perimeter of 18 units. Draw your new figure on grid paper. Show clearly where you added tiles to the pentomino.

B. What is the smallest number of tiles you can add to the pentomino to make a new figure with a perimeter of 18 units? Draw the new figure, showing where you would add tiles to the pentomino.

C. What is the largest number of tiles you can add to the pentomino to make a new figure with a perimeter of 18 units? Draw the new figure, showing where you would add tiles to the pentomino.

For parallelograms A–G, find the area and explain how you found it.

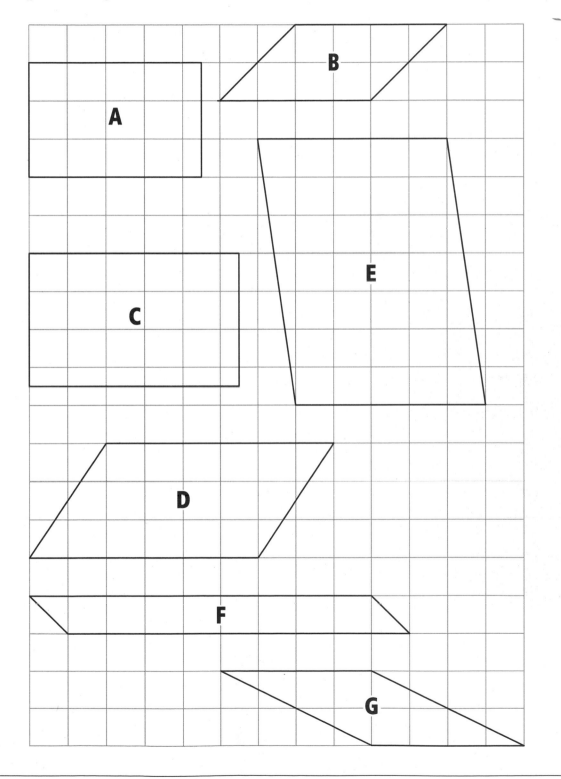

In A–E, make your drawings on centimeter grid paper. Note that cm is the abbreviation for centimeters, and cm² is the abbreviation for square centimeters.

A. Draw a rectangle with an area of 18 cm². Then, try to draw a different rectangle with an area of 18 cm². Do the rectangles have the same perimeter? If you couldn't draw a different rectangle, explain why.

B. Draw a rectangle with the dimensions 3 cm by 8 cm. Then, try to draw a different rectangle with these same dimensions. Do the rectangles have the same area? If you couldn't draw a different rectangle, explain why.

C. Draw a parallelogram with a base of 7 cm and a height of 4 cm. Then, try to draw a different parallelogram with these same dimensions. Do the parallelograms have the same area? If you couldn't draw a different parallelogram, explain why.

D. Draw a parallelogram with all side lengths equal to 6 cm. Then, try to draw a different parallelogram with all side lengths equal to 6 cm. Do the parallelograms have the same area? If you couldn't draw a different parallelogram, explain why.

E. Draw a parallelogram with an area of 30 cm². Then, try to draw a different parallelogram with the same area. Do the parallelograms have the same perimeter? If you couldn't draw a different parallelogram, explain why.

Draw two different nonrectangular parallelograms on a sheet of grid paper, and cut them out. Cut one of your parallelograms into two pieces so that the pieces can be reassembled to form a rectangle. Do the same for the second parallelogram. Use one of your parallelograms to complete parts A–C.

A. Record the base, height, perimeter, and area of the original parallelogram.

B. Record the length, width, perimeter, and area of the rectangle you made from the parallelogram pieces.

C. What relationships do you see between the measures for the rectangle and the measures for the parallelogram from which it was made?

For triangles A–H below, find the area and perimeter and explain how you found them.

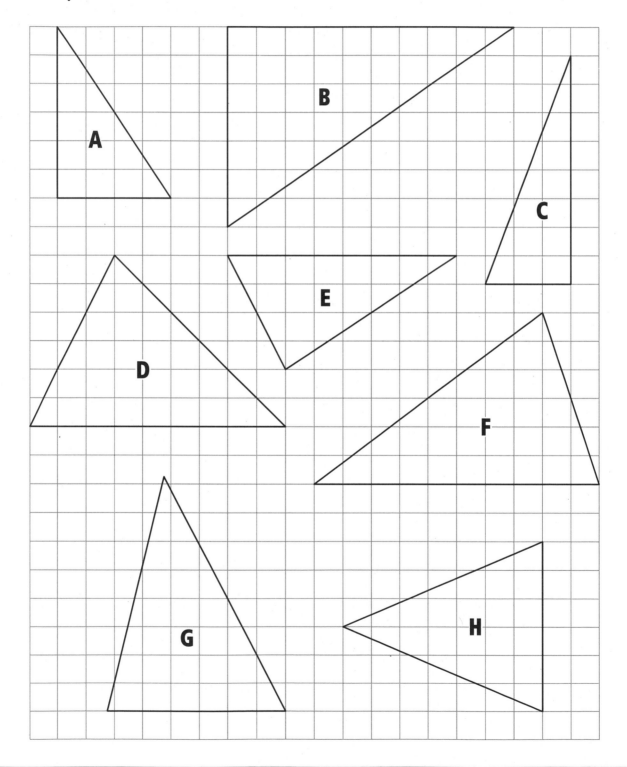

In A–D, make your drawings on centimeter grid paper. Remember that cm is the abbreviation for centimeters, and cm² is the abbreviation for square centimeters.

A. Draw a triangle with a base of 5 cm and a height of 6 cm. Then, try to draw a different triangle with these same dimensions. Do the triangles have the same area? If you couldn't draw a different triangle, explain why.

B. Draw a triangle with an area of 15 cm². Then, try to draw a different triangle with an area of 15 cm². Do the triangles have the same perimeter? If you couldn't draw a different triangle, explain why.

C. Draw a triangle with sides of length 3 cm, 4 cm, and 5 cm. Then, try to draw a different triangle with these same side lengths. Do the triangles have the same area? If you couldn't draw a different triangle, explain why.

D. A right triangle is a triangle that has a right angle. Draw a right triangle with a 30° angle. Then, try to draw a different right triangle with a 30° angle. Do the triangles have the same area? If you couldn't draw a different triangle, explain why.

Draw two triangles on a sheet of grid paper. Make sure the triangles are very different from one another. For each triangle, complete parts A–C.

A. Record the base, height, area, and perimeter of your triangle.

B. Make a copy of your triangle, and cut out both copies. Experiment with putting the two triangles together to make new polygons. Describe and sketch the polygons that are possible.

C. Can you make a parallelogram by piecing together the two identical triangles? If so, record the base, height, area, and perimeter of the parallelogram. How do these measures compare to the measures of the original triangles?

D. Draw a parallelogram on grid paper, and cut it out. Can you cut the parallelogram into two triangles that are the same shape and size? Describe and sketch what you find.

The Sole D'Italia Pizzeria sells small, medium, and large pizzas. A small is 9 inches in diameter, a medium is 12 inches in diameter, and a large is 15 inches in diameter. Prices for cheese pizzas are $6.00 for small, $9.00 for medium, and $12.00 for large.

A. Draw a 9-inch, a 12-inch, and a 15-inch "pizza" on centimeter grid paper. Let 1 centimeter of the grid paper represent 1 inch on the pizza. Estimate the radius, circumference, and area of each pizza. (You may want to use string to help you find the circumference.)

B. Which measurement—radius, diameter, circumference, or area—seems most closely related to price? Explain your answer.

In this problem, you will work with a collection of circular objects.

A. Use a tape measure to find the diameter and circumference of each object. Record your results in a table with these column heads.

Object	Diameter	Circumference

B. Make a coordinate graph of your data. Use the horizontal axis for diameter and the vertical axis for circumference.

C. Study your table and your graph, looking for patterns and relationships that will allow you to predict the circumference from the diameter. Test your ideas on some other circular objects. Once you think you have found a pattern, answer this question: What do you think the relationship is between the diameter and the circumference of a circle?

Find as many different ways as you can to estimate the area of the circle below. For each method, give your area estimate and carefully describe how you found it. Include drawings in your descriptions if they help show what you did.

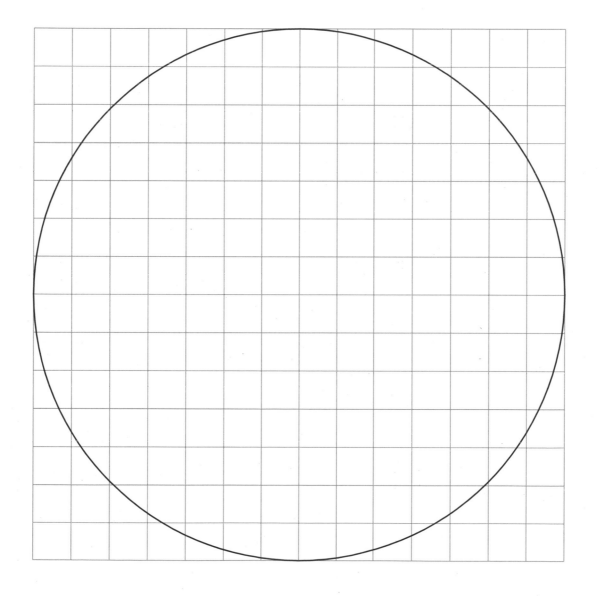

A. For each circle, cut out several copies of the radius square from a sheet of centimeter grid paper. Find out how many radius squares it takes to cover the circle. You may cut the radius squares into parts if you need to. Record your data in a table with these column headings:

Circle	Radius of circle	Area of radius square	Area of circle	Number of radius squares needed

B. Now draw a couple of your own circles on centimeter grid paper. You can use circles from the objects you measured in Problem 7.2 and from your Shapes Set. Make radius squares for each circle, and find out how many radius squares it takes to cover each circle. Add this data to your table.

C. Describe any patterns you see in your data.

D. If you were asked to estimate the area of any circle in "radius squares," what would you report as the best estimate?

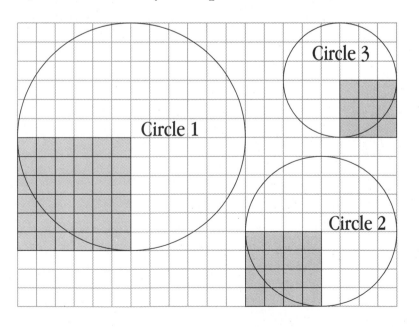

The following diagram shows the cross section of a damaged tree and the cross section of the new trees that will be planted to replace it.

Old tree

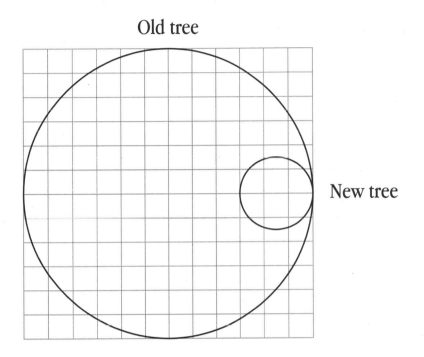

New tree

A. How many new trees must be planted if the diameter rule is applied?

B. How many new trees must be planted if the area rule is applied?

Dear Family,

The next unit in your child's course of study in mathematics class this year is *Covering and Surrounding*. Its focus is area and perimeter, and it teaches students to understand, find, and use perimeters and areas of rectangles, parallelograms, triangles, and circles. In addition, students use informal means (estimating and counting) to find areas and perimeters of nongeometric shapes.

In this unit, students use square tiles, transparent grids, and measuring tools to help find areas and perimeters in interesting and realistic situations. They also work to design shapes that fit certain conditions, and then determine whether more than one shape satisfies the conditions. These experiences add to the understanding students need to succeed in continued study of geometry and measurement.

By the end of this unit, your child will have developed rules for finding areas and perimeters of rectangles, parallelograms, triangles, and circles. Many ideas from the *Prime Time* unit will be revisited in this unit, especially the connection between factors and dimensions of rectangles.

You can help your child in several ways:

- Encourage him or her to use the measuring tools you have at home to practice making measurements. These tools might include measuring tapes, rulers, and metersticks.

- Help him or her develop personal referents for estimating lengths and distances. For example, the distance from home to school might be one mile, or the span of your child's hand might be six inches. Your child can use these referents to estimate other distances and lengths.

- Help your child develop personal referents for estimating area. For example, the area of his or her bedroom can be used to estimate areas of other rooms.

- Look over your child's homework and make sure all questions are answered and that explanations are clear.

As always, if you have any questions or concerns about this unit or your child's progress in the class, please feel free to call. All of us here are interested in your child and want to be sure that this year's mathematics experiences are enjoyable and promote a firm understanding of mathematics.

Sincerely,

Estimada familia,

La próxima unidad del programa de matemáticas de su hijo o hija para este curso se llama *Covering and Surrounding* (*Cubrir y rodear*). La misma trata principalmente sobre el área y el perímetro; en ella se enseña a los alumnos a comprender, hallar y utilizar los perímetros y las áreas de rectángulos, paralelogramos, triángulos y círculos. Además, los alumnos emplearán técnicas poco formalistas (la estimación y el conteo) para hallar dichas medidas en figuras no geométricas.

En la presente unidad los alumnos emplean fichas cuadradas, cuadrículas transparentes e instrumentos de medición para hallar en situaciones interesantes y realistas las áreas y los perímetros. También tratan de diseñar figuras que se ajusten a ciertas condiciones y luego determinar si más de una figura las satisface. Este tipo de experiencias les facilitan la comprensión que necesitan tener para poder seguir avanzando en el estudio de la geometría y las mediciones.

Una vez finalizada la unidad, su hijo o hija habrá creado reglas para hallar las áreas y los perímetros de rectángulos, paralelogramos, triángulos y círculos. Muchas ideas procedentes de la unidad *Prime Time* volverán a tratarse en esta unidad, en concreto la relación entre los factores y las dimensiones de los rectángulos.

Para ayudar a su hijo o hija, ustedes pueden hacer lo siguiente:

- Anímenle a practicar con los instrumentos de medición que tengan en casa, como pueden ser las cintas métricas, las reglas normales y las reglas de un metro.

- Ayúdenle a formar referencias personales para estimar longitudes y distancias. Así, por ejemplo, la distancia entre la casa y la escuela puede ser de una milla o el ancho de la mano abierta de su hijo o hija puede ser de seis pulgadas. Posteriormente, podrá usar las referencias para estimar otras distancias y longitudes.

- Ayúdenle a formar referencias personales para estimar el área. Así, por ejemplo, el área de su dormitorio puede utilizarse para estimar la de las demás habitaciones.

- Repasen su tarea para asegurarse de que conteste todas las preguntas y escriba con claridad las explicaciones.

Y como de costumbre, si ustedes necesitan más detalles o aclaraciones respecto a esta unidad o sobre los progresos de su hijo o hija en esta clase, no duden en llamarnos. A todos nos interesa su hijo o hija y queremos asegurarnos de que las experiencias matemáticas que tenga este año sean lo más amenas posibles y ayuden a fomentar en él o ella una sólida comprensión de las matemáticas.

Atentamente,

Half-Centimeter Grid Paper

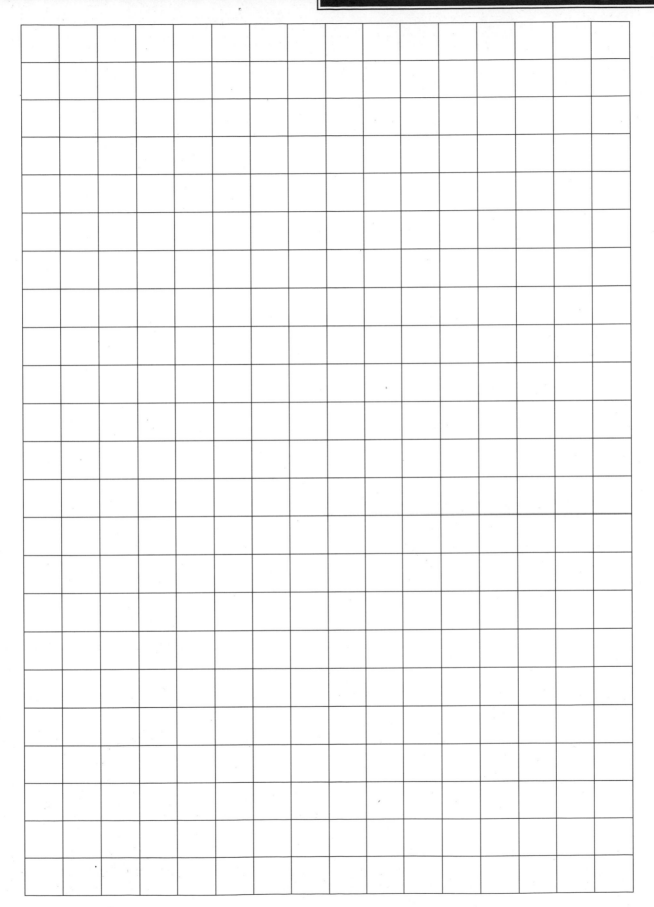

Covering and Surrounding

Quarter-Inch Grid Paper

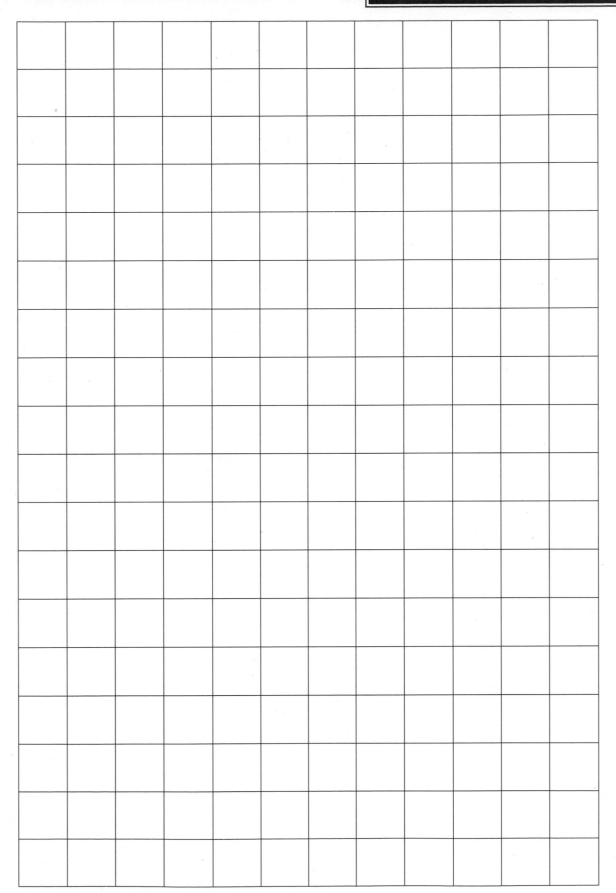

Additional Practice

Investigation 1

1. Find the area and the perimeter of each of the four shapes below.

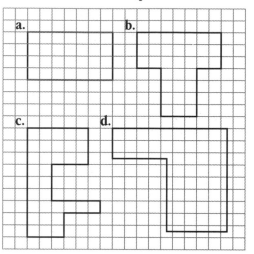

2. Susan is helping her father measure the living room floor because they want to buy new carpeting. The floor is in the shape of a rectangle with a width of 10 feet and a length of 14 feet.

   a. Draw a sketch that shows the shape of the floor and label the length and width.

   b. If the carpeting costs $1.75 per square foot, how much will it cost to buy the exact amount of carpeting needed to carpet the living room? Explain your reasoning.

   c. Base board needs to be installed along the base of the walls to hold the carpeting in place. Base board costs $2.35 per foot. There is one 6-foot wide entry into the living room that does not need base board. Find the exact amount of base board needed and the exact cost. Explain your reasoning.

3. Ellen drew a rectangle. She says the area of her rectangle is 7 square units and the perimeter is 16 units. Do you think Ellen is correct about the perimeter and area of her rectangle? Explain why or why not.

4. Use the diagram below to answer the following questions.

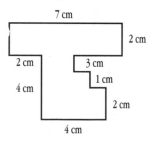

   a. What is the perimeter of the figure?

   b. What is the area of the figure?

   c. Explain how you found your answers for parts a and b.

Investigation 2

1. Use the diagram below to answer the following questions.

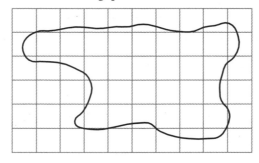

    a. Estimate the perimeter of the blob and explain your estimation strategy.

    b. Estimate the area of the blob and explain your estimation strategy.

    c. Do you think your estimates for a and b are larger or smaller than the exact perimeter and area? Explain your reasoning.

2. Use the diagram below to answer the following questions.

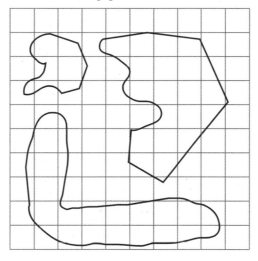

    a. Estimate the area that is covered by blobs. Explain your reasoning.

    b. Estimate the area that is *not* covered by blobs. Explain your reasoning.

    c. Someone claimed that the area of the grid covered by blobs is about 105 square units. Do you think this is a good estimate? Explain your reasoning.

    d. Someone claimed that the area not covered by blobs is about 10 square units. Do you think this is a good estimate? Explain your reasoning.

3. On a piece of grid paper, outline a 10×10 square. Inside the square draw a blob with an area of about 40 square units.

    a. Explain the method you used to draw your blob.

    b. Estimate the perimeter of your blob and explain your estimation strategy.

Investigation 3

1. Give the dimensions of the rectangle with an area of 100 square units and whole-number side lengths that has

    a. the largest perimeter.

    b. the smallest perimeter.

    c. Explain how you found your answers to parts a and b.

2. Jim has designed a rectangle with an area of 100 square feet and a perimeter of 401 feet.

    a. Is it possible that Jim's rectangle has whole-number side lengths? Explain your reasoning.

    b. What are the dimensions of Jim's rectangle?

3. Claire and Chad want to design a rectangular pen for their new puppy. They want the pen to have an area of 48 square feet. Fencing costs $0.85 per foot.

    a. What are the dimensions and the cost of the least expensive pen Claire and Chad could build, assuming the side lengths are whole numbers? Explain your reasoning.

    b. What are the dimensions and the cost of the most expensive pen Claire and Chad could build, assuming the side lengths are whole numbers? Explain your reasoning.

    c. Give the dimensions and the cost of a rectangular pen with whole-number side lengths and a cost between the least and most expensive pens you found in parts a and b.

    d. Of the three pens you found, which one would you suggest that Claire and Chad build? Explain your choice.

4. For each of the following, state whether the given perimeter is possible for a rectangle with an area of 42 square units and whole-number side lengths.

    a. 28 units   b. 46 units   c. 34 units   d. 41 units

Investigation 4

1. On a sheet of grid paper, draw all the possible rectangles with whole-number side lengths that have a perimeter of 10 units. Explain how you made sure you did not miss any possibilities in making your rectangles.

2. For each of the following, tell whether the given area is possible for a rectangle with a perimeter of 28 units and whole-number side lengths. Explain your reasoning.

   a. 24 square units   **b.** 40 square units   **c.** 42 square units   **d.** 45 square units

3. Tracy has 40 feet of material to make the perimeter of a rectangular sandbox for her little brother.

   a. What rectangle with whole-number side lengths would give the sandbox with the greatest area? Explain your reasoning.

   b. What rectangle with whole-number side lengths would give the sandbox with the least area? Explain your reasoning.

   c. Give the dimensions of a rectangle with whole-number side lengths that has an area between the least and greatest areas you found in parts a and b.

   d. Of the three rectangles you found, which one would you recommend that Tracy make? Explain your reasoning.

4. Travis has designed a rectangle with an area of 59 square units. His rectangle is the smallest rectangle (that is, the rectangle with smallest area) with whole-number side lengths that can be made from the perimeter of the rectangle.

   a. What are the length and width of the rectangle? Explain your reasoning.

   b. What is the perimeter of the rectangle? Explain your reasoning.

5. Helen has designed a rectangle with an area of 225 square units. Her rectangle is the largest rectangle (that is, the rectangle with largest area) with whole-number side lengths that can be made from the perimeter of the rectangle.

   a. What are the length and width of the rectangle? Explain your reasoning.

   b. What is the perimeter of the rectangle? Explain your reasoning.

Investigation 5

1. For each of the following, find the area and the perimeter of the parallelogram.

a.

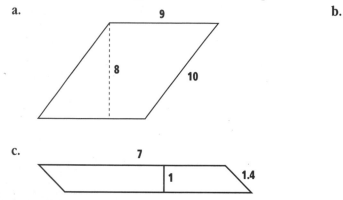

c.

b.

2. Use the diagram below to answer the following questions.

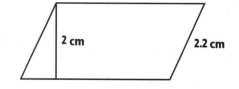

a. If the perimeter of the parallelogram is 14.4 centimeters, what is the length of the base? Explain your reasoning.

b. What is the area of the parallelogram? Explain your reasoning.

3. The area of a parallelogram is 24 square centimeters, and the base of the parallelogram is 6 centimeters.

a. What is the height of the parallelogram? Explain your reasoning.

b. If the perimeter of the parallelogram is 22 centimeters, what is the length of the other side of the parallelogram (that is, the side that isn't the base)? Explain your reasoning.

Investigation 6

1. Find the area and perimeter of each shape below.

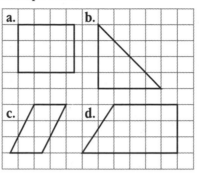

2. Find the area and perimeter of each shape below.

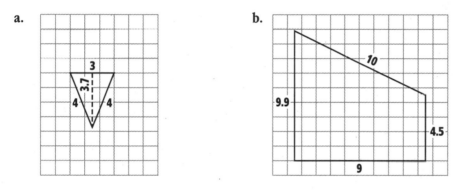

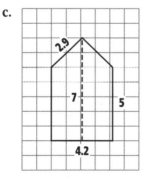

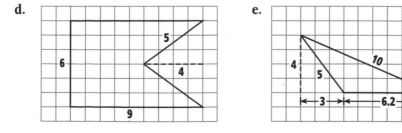

Investigation 7

1. For each of the following, find the circumference and the area of the circle.

    a.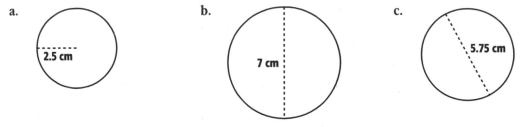
    2.5 cm

    b.
    7 cm

    c.
    5.75 cm

2. A circular cherry pie has a diameter of 11 inches and is cut into 8 equal-size pieces. What is the area of each piece of pie? Explain how you found your answer.

3. Use the diagram at the right to answer the following questions.

    a. What is the perimeter of the figure? Explain your reasoning.

    b. What is the area of the figure? Explain your reasoning.

    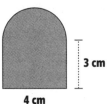
    3 cm
    4 cm

4. Use the diagram below to answer the following questions.

    a. What is the perimeter of the figure? Explain your reasoning.

    b. What is the area of the figure? Explain your reasoning.

    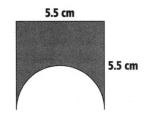
    5.5 cm
    5.5 cm

5. Below is a diagram of a jogging track. Use the diagram to answer the following questions.

    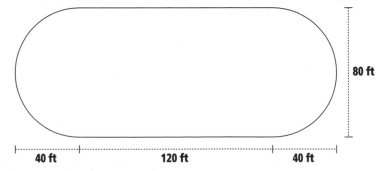
    80 ft
    40 ft   120 ft   40 ft

    a. What is the total distance around the jogging track? Explain your reasoning.

    b. How much area does the jogging track enclose? Explain your reasoning.

    c. If Tony wants to jog 4 miles, how many times will he have to jog around the track (remember that 5280 feet is 1 mile)? Explain your reasoning.

Answer Keys

Investigation 1

1. **a.** P = 22 units, A = 28 square units   **b.** P = 28 units, A = 33 square units

    c. P = 35 units, A = 33 square units   **d.** P = 36 units, A = 53.75 square units

2. **a.** Students should draw and label a 10 × 14 rectangle.   **b.** $245   **c.** $98.70

3. Ellen is correct, i.e., she drew a 1 × 7 rectangle.

4. **a.** 30 centimeters   **b.** 27 square centimeters

    c. Possible answers: Subdivide the figure into rectangles to find both the area and perimeter.

Investigation 2

1. **a.** The perimeter is about 25 units. The perimeter can be found by surrounding the figure with a piece of string, marking the distance on the string, and then using the grid to count the number of units.

    b. The area is about 30 square units. The area can be found by counting "whole" square units inside the blob and then "piecing together" more whole units from partial squares inside the blob.

    c. Possible answer: My answers are a little too big because I always rounded up when I was piecing together whole units or square units.

2. **a.** About 38 square units. The area can be found by using the "piecing together" strategy.

    b. The grid is 10 × 10, so about 100 − 38, or about 62 units are not covered by blobs.

    c. This is a bad overestimate. The entire grid has an area of only 100 square units, so blobs must cover less than 100 square units.

    d. This is a bad underestimate. You can easily see more than 10 square units on the grid not covered by blobs.

3. **a.** Possible answer: I enclosed, roughly, a 10 × 4 rectangle with the blob.

    b. Answers will vary.

Investigation 3

1. **a.** 1 × 100 rectangle   **b.** 10 × 10 rectangle

    c. For a given area, the longest, skinniest rectangle has the greatest perimeter and the most "square-like" rectangle has the least perimeter.

2. **a.** No, since largest perimeter with whole-number side lengths is 202 units for a 1 × 100 rectangle.

    b. 0.5 × 200

3. **a.** $23.80 for an 8 × 6 rectangle

    b. $83.30 for 1 × 48 rectangle

    c. Possible answer: A 4 × 12 pen would have a perimeter of 32 and cost $27.20.

    d. Possible answer: The 8 × 6 in part a would be best because it is the least expensive and provides the most space for the puppy to play.

4. **a.** Not possible   **b.** Yes, a 2 × 21 rectangle   **c.** Yes, a 3 × 14 rectangle   **d.** Not possible

Answer Keys

Investigation 4

1. Two are possible, a 1×4 and a 2×3.

2. **a.** Yes, a 2×12 rectangle   **b.** Yes, a 10×4 rectangle
   c. Not possible   **d.** Yes, a 9×5 rectangle

3. **a.** a 10×10 rectangle   **b.** a 1×19 rectangle   **c.** Possible answer: a 5×15 rectangle.
   d. Possible answer: the 10×10 because it is the most open for playing

4. **a.** 1×59 **b.** 120 units

5. **a.** 15×15 **b.** 60 units

Investigation 5

1. **a.** P = 38 units, A = 80 sq. units   **b.** P = 24 units, A = 32.4 sq. units
   c. P = 16.8 units, A = 7 sq. units

2. **a.** 5 cm   **b.** 10 sq. cm

3. **a.** 4 cm   **b.** 5 cm

Investigation 6

1. **a.** P = 13 units, A = 10.5 sq. units   **b.** P = 13.7 units, A = 8 sq. units
   c. P = 10.7 units, A = 6 sq. units   **d.** P = 16.6 units, A = 15 sq. units

2. **a.** P = 11 units, A = 5.55 sq. units   **b.** P = 33.4 units, A = 64.8 sq. units
   c. P = 20 units, A = 27.09 sq. units   **d.** P = 34.5 units, A = 42 sq. units
   e. P = 21.2 units, A = 12.4 sq. units

Investigation 7

1. **a.** C = 15.7 cm, A = 19.6 sq. cm   **b.** C = 22 cm, A = 38.5 sq. cm
   c. C = 18.1 cm, A = 26 sq. cm

2. Each slice of pie has an area of 11.9 sq. inches.

3. **a.** 16.28 cm   **b.** 18.28 sq. cm

4. **a.** 25.14 cm   **b.** 22.30 sq. cm

5. **a.** 491.3 ft   **b.** 14,627 sq. ft   **c.** about 43 times

area The measure of the amount of surface enclosed by the sides of a figure. To find the area of a figure, you can count how many unit squares it takes to cover the figure. You can find the area of a rectangle by multiplying the length by the width. This is simply a shortcut method for finding the number of unit squares it takes to cover the rectangle. If a figure has curved or irregular sides, you can estimate the area by covering the surface with a grid and counting whole grid squares and parts of grid squares. When the area of a shape is given, units, such as square feet or cm², should be included to indicate the size of the unit square that was used to find the area. The area of the square below is 9 square units, and the area of the rectangle is 8 square units.

circle A two-dimensional object in which every point is the same distance from a point (not on the circle) called the *center*. Point C is the center of the circle below.

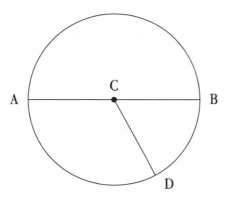

circumference The distance around (or perimeter of) a circle. It takes slightly more than three diameters to match the circumference of a circle. More formally, the circumference of a circle is *pi* (π) times the diameter of the circle. Pi is the mathematical name for the ratio of a circle's circumference to its diameter. This ratio is the same for every circle and is approximately equal to 3.1416.

diameter The maximum distance from one point on a circle to another point on the circle. A segment that goes from one point on a circle, through the center, to another point on the circle. In the circle shown in the description of "Circle," segment AB is a diameter.

linear dimensions Linear measurements, such as length, width, base, and height, which describe the size of figures. The longest dimension or the dimension along the bottom of a rectangle is usually called the *length*, and the other dimension is called the *width*, but it is not incorrect to reverse these labels. The word *base* is used when talking about triangles and parallelograms. The base is usually measured along a horizontal side, but it is sometimes convenient to think of one of the other sides as the base. For a triangle, the height is the perpendicular distance from the vertex opposite the base to the base. For a parallelogram, the height is the perpendicular distance from a point on the side opposite the base to the base. You need to be flexible when you encounter these terms, so you are able to determine their meanings from the context of the situation.

perimeter The measure of the distance around a figure. Perimeter is a measure of length. To find the perimeter of a figure, you count the number of unit lengths it takes to surround the figure. When the perimeter of a shape is given, units, such as centimeters, feet, or yards, should be included to indicate the unit length that was used to find the perimeter. The perimeter of the square above is 12 units, because 12 units of length (square sides) surround the figure. The perimeter of the rectangle is 18 units. Notice that the rectangle has a larger perimeter, but a smaller area, than the square.

perpendicular lines Lines that meet at right angles. The length and width of a rectangle are perpendicular to each other and the base and height of a triangle are perpendicular to each other. In diagrams, perpendicular lines are often indicated by drawing a small square where the lines meet.

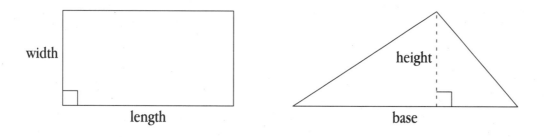

radius The distance from the center of a circle to a point on the circle. The radius is half of the diameter. A segment from the center of a circle to a point on the circle. In the circle above, CD is one radius. The plural of *radius* is *radii*. All the radii of a circle have the same length.

Index

Index

Index